Deare _____ lle,

THAT YOUR
JOY
MAY BE COMPLETE

So many thanks
for all you did for
me at Bernardsville
& the Mother-House.

Prayerfully
yours,

Fr. George, S.J.

Available from the same author and publisher:

BE FILLED WITH THE FULLNESS OF GOD
Living in the Indwelling Trinity
ISBN 1-56548-024-4, paper, 144 pp.

George Maloney

THAT YOUR JOY

MAY BE COMPLETE

The Secret of Becoming A Joyful Person

New City Press

Dedicated to
Dolores Wysocki
who has known deep sufferings but through them
knows the true experience of Christian joy.

Sincere thanks to
Sr. Mary Faith, O.S.B., June Culver
and Frances Phelan for their help.

New City Press, 202 Cardinal Rd., Hyde Park, NY 12538
©1994 George Maloney
Printed in the United States

Cover art by D. Assmus

Imprimi Potest:
Bert R. Thelen, S.J.
Provincial of the Society of Jesus
Wisconsin Province

Library of Congress Cataloging-in-Publication Data:

Maloney, George A., 1924-
    That your joy may be complete : the secret of becoming a joyful
person / George Maloney.

    Includes bibliographical references.
    ISBN 1-56548-062-7 : $8.95
    1. Joy—Religious aspects—Christianity.   2. Christian life—
Catholic authors.   I. Title.
BV4647.J68M35   1994
241'.4—dc20   93-47943

Contents

Introduction

Would you consider yourself to be a joyful person? Sometimes, you might reply. Why not always joyful as Paul encouraged the early Christians of Philippi: "Rejoice in the Lord always. I shall say it again: rejoice!" (Ph 4:4)?

Would you say we Americans as a whole are a very joyful people? We desperately seek happiness but end up in loneliness and meaninglessness to our lives since we place our happiness not in God but in the possession of more "things" that bring us pleasure and a false security.

Would you agree with me that we as Christians do not excel in rejoicing always and in being a joy to all others? We are as sad and worrisome as other citizens of our country, not allowing our Christian beliefs to be lived out in the true sign that we are disciples of Jesus Christ, that we love one another as he loved us, and that we radiate the joy of his Holy Spirit in all our relationships toward God and neighbor.

The proof of how matured we are as Christians and as fully realized human beings is measured by how much we have allowed God's perfect love to transform us. This divine love that should abound in our hearts through the Spirit given to us (Rm 5:5) is always accompanied by the visible gift of the Spirit of joy (Ga 5:22).

I was shocked to find in the libraries I consulted how few books have dealt with Christian joy. There were books with titles such as: *Joy in Sex; Joy in Living According to Your Potential; Joy in Computers*, etc. Why so few books on true Christian joy?

So you will excuse me for my audacity in writing such a book. My purpose in this book is to approach the topic of Christian joy in the light of our Christian faith that roots joy as a gift of the Holy

Spirit that is based on the intimate, loving relationships between the divine triune persons and ourselves. It is nearest to and accompanies true love. Such joy no trials, no suffering, not even death can ever take from us! "Rejoice in the Lord always" (Ph 4:4).

Authentic Christian joy is a sign of the living and loving presence of the Trinity community of love, gifting us with a share in their eternal joy. Jesus is the *way* that leads us to this eternal joy. He redeems us from all sin and death, and through the baptism of water and his Spirit we become divinized children of God the Father by grace. Through the death and resurrection of Jesus Christ, the Word of God made flesh, and the outpouring of the Holy Spirit into our hearts, we receive the gift of the Spirit's joy that flows from the love of God that abounds in our hearts through the Spirit given to us (Rm 5:5).

Such Christian joy makes it possible to bear suffering and even death in a continued joy. "Not only that, but we even boast of our afflictions, knowing that affliction produces endurance, and endurance, proven character, and proven character, hope, and hope does not disappoint" (Rm 5:3-4). This allows us to be a visible sign of joy to others, as joyful love brings forth an openness to all we meet to be available in joyful service to live for their happiness.

Right teaching leads to right living

We need to understand true Christian joy by our prayerful reflection upon God's revelation since right teaching, *orthodoxia,* must lead to right *praxis,* right living: *orthopraxis.* The immanently indwelling Trinity as emptying love for us, as revealed by Jesus Christ and the Holy Spirit, is the beginning and the ultimate source of any lasting joy, both in this life and in the life to come.

In his humanity Jesus is the image of the invisible God (Col 1:15). He invites us in the gospels to live lives of joy as he did, especially joy in loving service to others. Jesus is the joy of our desires, as we contemplate all things in the Word of God made flesh, in whom all creatures have their being. We are to discover in the gospels how to live in harmony with Jesus Christ according to whose image and likeness we have been created (Gn 1:26-27).

Christian joy requires us to enter into a process of continued conversion away from the brokenness within us and our false ego to find joy through our inner weeping and crying for the healing power of Jesus our Savior.

Jesus Christ gives us his own mother, Mary, to be our human archetype of how we, who make up the Church, can also be full of joy as Mary was on this earth and is now in glory.

A humble joy

True Christian joy must be real and not nebulous, practical in its manifestations, and not merely an ephemeral emotional "high" that is deflated at the first sign of trials and tribulations. Joy, therefore, must be founded in true humility that governs all our thoughts, words and deeds in our relationships to God, neighbor and God's entire creation.

Joy is most purified and shines out to others through suffering that brings us into the challenge to live in self-emptying love, which always will be accompanied by suffering, especially as we strive to die to our own self-centeredness and to place God Trinity as the true center of our being.

Such joy reaches its peak in the pass-over experience in our dying as we learn to surrender ourselves in childlike abandonment to God's holy and loving presence. We are prepared to enter into life after this life through the gifted source of joy, not always highly developed in the lives of many Christians while they live on this earth, namely, the joy of walking in the joyful and loving presence and intercession of God's angels and saints.

In the last two chapters, by way of summary of the joy we experience during our earthly pilgrimage and in the glorious life to come, we reflect on Jesus risen, our true joy and the gift of joy that Jesus and his Father give us, namely, the Holy Spirit. Joy is the

Spirit's gift to us when the love of God is experienced as abounding in our hearts through the Spirit who is God's gift of love as the binding and unifying power within the Trinity. He makes all joy possible, as our spirit and God's Spirit bear united witness that we are children of God and heirs of heaven with Christ Jesus (Rm 8:15).

To avoid seeing joy as a virtue which we mistakenly might think we can bring about by our own efforts, I added an epilogue, by way of summarizing the purpose of this work, to present the essential elements of a Christian theology of joy.

I pray these pages might ignite in the heart of you, reader, an ardent desire, both affectively and effectively, to experience that which Paul held out to the early Christians of Philippi:

> Rejoice in the Lord always. I shall say it again: rejoice! Your kindness should be known to all. The Lord is near. Have no anxiety at all. (Ph 4:4-6)

George Maloney

In Search of True Joy

Would you agree with me from your own personal experience that few persons in our modern society experience an abiding true joy, that which is the simultaneous expression of physical, psychological and spiritual integration? Such a deep and continued joy is the result of a harmony in our relationships with God, neighbor and the physical world around us.

Do you wish to know by a quick and infallible sign just how matured you are as a human being? If God is love and we have received our existence out of his triune community of love, we ought to be transformed by his indwelling love through his Spirit of love. But the proof of how much we have experienced God's beauty and love is measured by the fruit of the Holy Spirit dwelling within us. This fruit is "love, joy, peace, patience, kindness, goodness, trust-fulness, gentleness and self-control" (Ga 5:22).

Love does not exist except in a person actually loving someone else in self-emptying service. But such love does manifest itself infallibly by the signs of the Holy Spirit transforming us into loving human beings who love God with our whole heart and love our neighbor as we love ourselves (Mt 22:37-40). Such true love can be measured in our lives by the degree of joy and peaceful harmony we experience in our hearts, which we manifest externally toward others in all our relationships toward them.

Lack of joy

Yet can we Christians really say we are habitually always joyful persons? Do we not become upset as much as non-Christians do over the least things that have power to change us into angry, unhappy,

11

agitated persons? How often I hear persons complaining how upset, even angry, they become because the weather is so "unpleasant," or the food in a restaurant is not to their liking. Griping, complaining, yielding to angry moods are more common to us, is it not true, than an habitually deep, calm joy and inner harmony.

Mistaken notions of joy

Perhaps one main reason why we do not understand true joy and do not move toward living in such joy is that theologians and preachers have for centuries treated joy in a rational, analytical manner as did Thomas Aquinas. Following the teaching of Aristotle, Aquinas and other scholastic theologians schooled in the writings of Thomas taught that joy is one of the eleven basic passions or emotions (*Summa Theologiae,* Prima Primae, 23, 1, 4). Joy is attained as a pleasant state of quiescence in the good that is possessed.

Yet there is another way, which I hope to follow in this present work on joy, and that is to approach it in the light of our Christian faith that roots joy in intimate, loving relationships between self-giving persons to each other. Christian joy in the New Testament is not considered as a human virtue that we human beings are able to develop by certain ascetical techniques and exercises, whereby we act joyfully until we at last acquire joy as a permanent virtue, a good habit! Joy is not one of many emotions that we bring about by our own efforts, a peaceful, pleasurable state of being.

Joy is a sign of loving presence between persons. It is nearest to true love and therefore is sheer gift given and received, but not acquired by our own efforts. Joy is seen in scripture as not so much our own doing, but ultimately and most perfectly is offered to us as a gift of God, whereby we know through the Spirit that God Trinity gives itself to us as individual persons in one nature of divine love as free gift.

Another mistaken notion about joy is that it is a created thing rooted solely in our emotions. In this we can be often deceived, especially when we make joy synonymous with pleasures. Plato knew in the fourth century before Christ that true joy and lasting happiness could never be the same as pleasure. The majority of modern people judge happiness mainly by the amount of pleasure we may or may not be experiencing at any given moment. The worldly-minded person seeks joy that can only be illusionary in physical or psychological pleasures of the body or mind, in things that give to the individual person a sense of independent power.

True joy can never consist in having perishable pleasures. Authentic joy can never be found in "having" things or power to control others by exploitation, but only in giving of oneself to others in loving service. Joy begets new life in others and is never hoarding into "barns," as Jesus taught in the gospels. It is discovered in sharing ourselves with others.

To be joyful is to acknowledge a fullness of life, of perfection and power received as a gift of God's loving presence. Otherwise we become victimized by our own self-centeredness. We in our false selves will always be bandied about like a reed in the desert blown by the wind, like a yo-yo that goes up and down, manipulated by someone or something outside of ourselves.

The Christian secret of joy

If we call ourselves Christians, we must observe from the life of Christ and his teachings lived out by his serious followers, the saints, that there can be the fruit of the Holy Spirit who brings us a joy that no sufferings, tribulations or afflictions, not even death itself, can ever take from us (Rm 8:35).

Paul recalls to his early Christian converts in Thessalonica: "And you became imitators of us and of the Lord, receiving the word in great affliction, with joy from the Holy Spirit" (1 Thes 1:6). How, you might ask, is it possible for you to experience joy even when there is no pleasure, but just the opposite, great pain and suffering? Perhaps the story of Blessed John Tauler may help us to understand Christian joy as possible even in great suffering, even death.

Blessed John Tauler, the fourteenth century Rhenish mystic and Dominican theologian, prayed for eight years that God would send him a person who would be able to point out to him the true way to perfection. One day while he was in prayer, Tauler felt this desire come over him very strongly. He heard a voice from within him urging him to go to the steps of the church, and there he would meet such a teacher.

Tauler found on the steps of the church a beggar in rags, with feet bare, wounded and caked with mud. He greeted the beggar with the words: "May God give you a good day" to which the beggar answered: "I do not remember ever having had a bad day." Tauler asked the beggar to explain how it was that he never had a bad day, never had been anything but happy. The beggar answered:

> You wished me a good day, and I answered that I cannot recall having ever spent a bad day. For, when famishing with hunger, I praise God equally; when I am in want, when I am rebuffed and despised, I still praise God; and consequently, I know not what it is to have a bad day. You next wished me a good and happy life, and I replied that I have never been otherwise than happy. That is perfectly true. For I have learned how to live with God, and I am convinced that whatever he does must necessarily be very good. Hence, everything which I receive from God, or which he permits that I receive from others, prosperity or adversity, sweet or bitter, I regard as a particular favor, and I accept it with joy from his hand. Besides, it is my first resolution never to attach myself to anything but the will of God alone. I have so merged my own will in his that whatsoever he wills, I will also. Therefore, I have been always happy.

The beggar had given all for *all* and had found the secret of true and ultimate happiness. It consists in perfect childlike abandonment to the heavenly Father's will in all circumstances of life. It is the joining of such surrender to profound humility and a return of self-sacrificing love to God, who has "emptied" himself in Jesus Christ for love of each of us individuals. This is the shortest road to mature human living and the secret of real joy.

A stable joy: gift of the Spirit

Our faith tells us that the Spirit of the risen Lord Jesus dwells within us always (Rm 8:9; 1 Col 6:19). We cannot always be happy or at least feel happy, especially in times of suffering. Yet, Paul assures us that we Christians should always rejoice. "Rejoice in the Lord always. I shall say it again: rejoice!" (Ph 4:4).

> So you also are now in anguish. But I will see you again, and your hearts will rejoice, and no one will take your joy away from you. (Jn 16:22)

Again Jesus said to his disciples: "I have told you this, so that my own joy may be in you and your joy be complete" (Jn 15:11). Such Christian joy, the gift of the Holy Spirit indwelling us, is grounded in the faith given us by the Spirit to believe that Jesus is truly the second person of the Trinity, and for love of us he became incarnate. He freely died for us to image the infinite, perfect love of the Father for us. Through the Spirit the Father and Son send into our hearts, we know Jesus has been raised from the dead and now lives with the Father and the Holy Spirit within us as the giver to us of a new creation, of new life in greatest abundance (2 Co 5:17-18).

Such joy is a mark of the living and loving presence of a community of love, the Trinity, giving us a share in their own eternal joy. Our joy, therefore, is our response to God's gift of himself as self-emptying Father through his self-giving Son in their mutual Spirit of love. Our being open to receive this gift is what it means to be truly religious and above all truly Christian. To be joyful as a Christian is to acknowledge a fullness in one's life, a fullness of perfection and power received as a gift of God's indwelling presence as triune community of self-sacrificing love.

Jesus rejoices always in the Father

Before we can see how Jesus is the cause of our stable Christian joy, we must turn to him and see how in his humanity he received joy from the Father through the Spirit so that he could joyfully give us himself as a gift of love, a eucharistic sacrifice on the cross, even unto death.

Within the Trinity, the Father "passes" over in giving himself completely to the Son (Col 2:9) in the Spirit. The Father loses himself as he lives for the happiness of the other, his only begotten Son. The Son has perfect joy because he is wholly giving back himself to the Father for the complete joy of the Father in the same Spirit of love.

In the incarnation Jesus Christ still remains one in the same nature as the Father, full of perfect joy. Yet, possessing our own human nature, Jesus had to learn how to live in each event of each moment in a joyful way, as you and I must learn to give the Father complete control of his life in all details. Joy is the experience of surrendering totally to God's love as we give ourselves in self-sacrificing love to him and our neighbor.

Jesus in the gospels shows us that his growth in joy took place slowly and in an unspectacular way as must our own individual growth in childlike trust in God. When Jesus gave himself up to the Father's will in the details of his concrete, human situation, it was a joyful act of freedom to take his life into his hands and return it totally and freely to his Father, the source of all his being.

Jesus: cause of our joy

Because Jesus, the Word made flesh for love of us, is God's perfect love in human form unto self-emptying death for us, he *saves,* redeems us from all sin and death. He baptizes us by water and the Spirit. He inserts us into his very own divine sonship before the Father. He reconciles us to God's fulfilling plan that the Father had conceived for our eternal happiness for all eternity (Eph 1:4 ff).

Jesus brings us joy by forgiving us all our sins. He is the Lamb of

God who takes away our sins (Jn 1:29-30). He makes this joy possible through our living encounter with the risen Jesus in the sacrament of reconciliation. But above all, our joy in God's joyful gifting of the Trinity to us reaches its fullness when we participate in the sacrament of the eucharist.

He sends us and continually releases for us the Holy Spirit who dwells within us. This Spirit gives us love, joy and peace that no one can ever take from us. Jesus is the reason we can rejoice always because he shares his resurrectional new life with us. He promised to give us his joy by the abiding presence of the Father, Son and Holy Spirit.

> I shall ask the Father,
> and he will give you another Advocate
> to be with you for ever,
> that Spirit of truth
> whom the world can never receive
> since it neither sees nor knows him;
> but you know him,
> because he is with you, he is in you.

(John 14:16-17)

Jesus promised that with the Spirit he would give us his own peace. "Peace I leave with you; my peace I give to you. Not as the world gives do I give it to you. Do not let your hearts be troubled or afraid" (Jn 14:27).

The risen Lord Jesus, through the outpouring Spirit, gives us faith, hope and love that the entire Trinity dwells with us. Heaven is already within us! We are sharers, even now, of the risen life of Jesus. We must not fear or be afraid of anything, not even death, for he has conquered all enemies and now gives us a share in his glorious, eternal life. "We were indeed buried with him through baptism into death, so that, just as Christ was raised from the dead by the glory of the Father, we too might live in newness of life" (Rm 6:14).

Joy: the mark of matured love

If we are to live always joyfully, we must learn how to suffer in joy, for joy comes as a fruit of true love, and without suffering there can be no authentic love. Paul tells us how through suffering we arrive at love: "Not only that, but we even boast of our afflictions, knowing that affliction produces endurance, and endurance, proven character, and proven character, hope, and hope does not disappoint, because the love of God has been poured out into our hearts through the Holy Spirit that has been given to us" (Rm 5:3-5).

If we wish to have a part with Christ, we must deny whatever in us prevents us from loving him in every thought, word and deed. We must put on his mind:

> You should put away the old self of your former way of life, corrupted through deceitful desires, and be renewed in the spirit of your minds, and put on the new self, created in God's way in righteousness and holiness in truth. (Eph 4:22-24)

In a way that is paradoxical we must forget trying to possess joy, and we will find it by being ready to accept all, even suffering, in order to be one with Christ, the cause of our everlasting joy. "All I want is to know Christ and the power of his resurrection and to share his suffering by reproducing the pattern of his death. That is the way I can hope to take my place in the resurrection of the dead. Not that I have become perfect yet: I have not yet won, but I am still running, trying to capture the prize for which Christ Jesus captured me. I can assure you, my brothers, I am far from thinking that I have already won. All I can say is that I forget the past and I strain ahead for what is still to come; I am racing for the finish, for the prize to which God calls us upwards to receive in Christ Jesus" (Ph 3:10-15 NJB).

Be a gift of joy to others

If we are to be the extension of Jesus Christ risen, then, to the degree that we rejoice in the gift of God's Spirit of joy indwelling us, to that degree the Holy Spirit pours out through us the gift of joy to others, to whom we are sent to become joy to them as we lovingly serve them. "And it is plain that you are a letter from Christ, drawn up by us, and written not with ink but with the Spirit of the living God, not on stone tablets, but on the tablets of your living hearts" (2 Co 3:3).

Deep down in all human beings God has implanted the burning desire to be joyful and radiant in an everlasting happiness that nothing can ever take away from us. But how can people around us ever believe in such divine love that generates this everlasting joy, unless they see us as radiant joy in all our actions and words before them, and we become for them a gift of joy?

Such joyful love demands an openness to all whom we meet, so that we are available in joyful readiness to live for their happiness. To be so available we must look upon all others with a joyful hope in their innate goodness. It is a call to a mutuality of an *I-Thou* relationship. Yet this necessitates our readiness to die to selfishness and to embrace the suffering out of which joy can emerge and flow out as gift to others.

In the beginning God was joy

These introductory pages can serve us as a general summary of what constitutes Christian joy. Now we can develop a solid theological foundation for more fully understanding Christian joy. Here we must begin to lay our foundation in a prayerful manner by beginning with what joy means between the Father and Son through their hidden, self-emptying love, the Spirit.

Then we can in greater detail examine the joy of Jesus Christ, the incarnate Word of God, which he developed in his human consciousness while living on this earth. It is this joy which he offers to us through his Spirit by inviting us to ground ourselves in his gospel values, which he preached and lived, and through which he calls us to share even now in his joy in this life of ours.

The joy of Jesus and his Father, given to us by their Spirit of love, is not a mere promise or hope to be given to us in the life to come. It is the gift of God's full joy in the future, eternal life, but already made ours in this life as we empty ourselves in order to be filled with the joy of Jesus in greater and greater abundance.

God: A Joyful Community

All of us human beings crave intimacy in loving relationships between ourselves and others. We possess a primal desire that stretches us always outward toward communion, union with others, but ultimately and fully with God. This is an inner drive propelling us to stretch out beyond the limited, self-contained levels of consciousness that lock us into a static, non-growth non-meaningfulness. This is a process of unending discovery of our true self, transformed by another's unselfish love for us.

Our lives become boring, jaded, turned in upon ourselves in unhappy loneliness until we enter into a oneness with another being in love. We begin to discover true joy only through the death to our self-containment, as we pass-over to take the risk to live for the happiness of another person.

We are wild animals prowling through the dark mazes of our unconscious, searching desperately for someone to love us and tame us into the joy and peace God calls us to enjoy as harbingers of receiving a participation in his beauty and love when we love others and they return that love to us. Thus we constantly are stretching out toward loving communion to find someone who will call us into our unique being by his or her committed love for us.

Yet, even the love we receive from other human beings will always leave us in a state of restless longing for a beauty that never fades, a joy that never turns to sadness. This is the revelation and strength of Christianity that Jesus Christ brings to us, namely, that we have come into being and are constantly being invited, ravished and drawn into a deeper sharing of God's own joyful community through Jesus Christ, the eternal Son of God made man in his Spirit of love and joy (Ga 5:22).

Ecstatic joy in the Trinity

The awesome transcendent God in his essence can never be comprehended by our natural powers of intellect. Yet, Jesus Christ assures us, that as he has come out of the triune community of joyful, self-sacrificing love of Father, Son and Holy Spirit, so in him and through his Spirit we can truly experience this transcendent Trinity as immanently dwelling within us and humbly sharing their unique selves with us. This indwelling Trinity as emptying love for us is the ultimate source of any lasting joy we may possess in this life and in the life to come.

Let us examine from Christ's revelation the joy within the Trinity that becomes the shared joy with us, as we live in total surrender to the indwelling Trinity in us. There is a beautiful word used by the early Eastern Fathers, especially Pseudo-Dionysius of the fifth century and Maximus the Confessor of the seventh century. This is the Greek word *ekstasis*. We would loosely translate it as *ecstasy*, but again, just as we so readily confuse joy with ecstatic pleasures, so we might miss the full meaning of divine ecstasy.

This refers to the burning love that bursts out from the Father without any barriers toward the Son through the self-emptying love, the Holy Spirit, and of the Son in returning love to the Father. It refers to the joyful discovering of the uniqueness of the Father only in the intimate relationship with the Son in self-gift to him through his Spirit. Here we see the beginning of what true joy means. It is out of the overflow that is the result of complete pass-over into the other with the losing of one's self-possession and the paradoxical finding of the true self in the loving gift of the other. Joy can never be separated from such ecstatic outpouring of oneself to live for the other.

Gabriel Marcel, the French philosopher, has well summarized this in his succinct statement: "The *I* is the child of the *We*." Love breaks down the barriers, and in "ecstasy," or a standing out of our habitual control, we surrender to live for the happiness of the other. In the Trinity each person exists in loving relationship toward another. The

Father discovers his unique personhood as Father only in begetting the Son through the Spirit of love. The Son discovers his *I-ness* only as he surrenders and calls the Father, *Abba,* and lives in love for him in and through the same Spirit of love. The Holy Spirit's *I-ness* is the procession of personified love as an expression of mutual self-giving love between the Father and the Son. For us to pray deeply in the heart is to experience this immense circulation of love among the persons within the divine family, drawing us in that same community of love.

Infinite zero

How feeble is our understanding of the ecstatic joy that must flow from all eternity between the heavenly Father and the Son in the *kenotic* or self-emptying love of the Spirit! The great Christian mystics penetrated somewhat into this trinitarian joy of the divine *I-Thou* in a *We* community through living in total self-emptying love as the ecstatic joy in their earthly lives. Above all in times of suffering and even death, they attested to their sharing in the trinitarian joy between the Father and Son in the same Spirit as they bore all in the Spirit's gift of joy.

Such mystics referred to God as the *Godhead,* the absolutely unknowable God, prior to a loving movement of person to person, as the Abyss, the Desert, the Wilderness, the Absolute beyond any being. This is motionless unity and balanced stillness. It is the fullness of being that has not yet spilled out in loving gift. In this state there is no experienced joy but only an infinite possibility of joy.

When the spark of love shoots through the darkened Void, it sets up a movement of desire. The dark side of God's "no-thingness" bursts into light, as God wishes to know himself in another. The Void wishes to come forth and express itself in love and thus discover the experience of joy. The Father wishes to know and love himself in his Son. He wishes to express and communicate himself by a word, a word that would give full expression to that infinite mind and thrill that mind in ecstatic, joyful union as Father and Son in love, the Spirit.

God's joyful family

The Father pours out himself in his Spirit of love totally into his Son. As the Son receives this perfect gift of the Father and thrills at becoming the unique Son of so beautiful a Father, he says his eternal, joyful yes back to the Father in the same Spirit of love. The three persons in ecstasy of union find perfect repose that we can call perfect joy.

Yet such repose, harmony, integration, joy within the Trinity can never be static idleness. Love within the heart of the Trinity is a motionless movement outward to share this realized unity of love with others. This infinite joy cannot be held within the Trinity, but the Trinity wishes to share this exuberant joy in sharing their very own divine nature with us human beings, created in God's image and likeness (Gn 1:26-27).

The love of God in three persons, bursting forth from within to pour itself outwardly into millions and millions of created beings, is the source of all creation and the source of all created joy. That which we discover of God's self-giving as Father, Son and Holy Spirit within the Trinity through revelation is the basis of the same trinitarian activity throughout our material world.

Our faith assures us that such ecstatic love of the Trinity explodes out through the same Spirit of love to be toward us, "empty receptacles" to be filled with God's goodness. How exciting and yet how humbling to realize that we, with the whole material creation, are caught up into the trinitarian ecstasy of love! We are a part of God's joyful discovery of what it means to be uniquely a Father toward a Son in the Spirit of love but also of what it means that he becomes our Father, as we live in Jesus Christ, his only begotten Son made flesh for love of us, in his Spirit.

As the Father is turned toward the Son in total openness, availability, vulnerability unto complete self-emptying, so the Son is turned in the same joyful Love, the Spirit, to the Father. That ecstatic "turning" to each other in love cannot be a different turning in love toward us. God has created us out of his mutual trinitarian joy that we might live also in ecstatic joy in going out of ourselves and moving always in loving presence to the Father, as we live in oneness with his Son Jesus Christ in the Holy Spirit as well as toward others.

As true joy comes in inter-personal relationships within the Trinity, so God Trinity enjoys a similar ecstatic joy in self-giving to us. The Father is full of joy in the Trinity in his self-giving totally to the Son (Col 2:9). Yet the Father is also completed in full joy as he receives his uniqueness as Father of his only begotten Son in the self-giving of the Son to the Father.

A humble, waiting God

In a similar way can we not boldly believe that God the Father humbly sets himself up to receive joy from our return of the total gift he makes of himself to us through his Son in his Spirit of love? He wants us to share in his fullness of joy. Yet, God knows in the trinitarian relations that each person gives in joy but also receives in joy from the other persons. So the same personalized relationships continue in their relationships to us in the history of salvation.

The heavenly Father humbly waits for the free gift of ourselves, and thus he receives joy beyond the joy he possesses in giving himself to us. We begin in some shadowy way to see that joy necessitates the possibility of suffering, since it is rooted in inter-personalized relationships. Especially we see this in our own personal history when we have freely refused to return the gifts of the Father, Son and Spirit by our own total self-emptying gift of love of ourselves back to God.

We need to turn to the incarnate Word, Jesus Christ, in order to see how God Trinity rejoices when we in joy (cost what it may in terms of the cross) offer ourselves in loving God with our whole heart (Dt 6:7) and loving other human persons in a gift of joyful self-sacrificing love to serve their happiness, as Jesus Christ lived in his earthly life.

A Valentine heart

Saint Valentine's Day,
a day for lovers
to remember
that love means death,
that love means a giving
of self to another
who becomes more important
than your own self.

This is a day to recall
the heart of you, O my God.
No one has ever loved
as you love me.
No one has ever suffered
so much in pained heart
as you who have given me
all in the love of Jesus emptied.

O Jesus!
Yours is the heart
closest to the heart of the Father.
Your pierced and empty heart
mirrors for me the self-emptying
of the Father's love for me.
He knows in you
that love is pain.
It is suffering.

It is death.
It is self-forgetting.
It is living for the other.
It is truly a pierced heart,
emptied of all from within.

O, Father and Son,
pour into my heart
your humble Spirit
of gentleness and patience,
of love, peace and joy,
that I, too, may learn
to love with your love
the other selves, my true selves
that you have gifted me
to love as I love myself.
May my heart offered to them
become a pierced heart,
a suffering heart,
as I slowly learn that love is death,
but it is also true, joyful life!

G.A.M.

A Joyful Jesus

I remember seeing a movie several years ago about the life of Christ in which there was a scene in which Jesus joins his disciples in playing a game similar to our modern day volleyball. It made me wonder whether Jesus ever joined in playing with youngsters or young men his own age. Surely the scene in the movie made me realize how rarely we picture Jesus as a normal person who would have enjoyed the leisure (and the fun of it all!) and joyfulness of playful moments with others, even to the point of dancing a good old-fashioned Jewish *hora* from time to time, especially at weddings.

Did you ever notice how in the history of Christianity so many different images of Jesus have been in vogue, seemingly to fit the way human beings in a Christian world wished to view themselves? Malachi Martin offers a list of such images of Jesus held by Christians at various periods of history. Besides the non-Christian Jesus images of Jesus-Jew (from about 50 A.D.) and Jesus-Muslim (from about the seventh century A.D.), pre-Reformation Christians developed the images of Jesus-Torquemada (of the Inquisition).

After the Protestant Reformers, Jesus-figures developed for the emotional needs of human beings against the sternness of dry-bone theologies a romantic, pious Jesus. In the nineteenth and twentieth centuries we find the Jesus-Jehovah's Witness, Jesus-Christian Scientist, Jesus-Original Gospel Movement, Jesus Pentecostalist, Jesus-Jesusite and Jesus-Yogi. For the more "reasonable" person there evolved such types as Jesus-Apollo, Jesus-Goodfellow, Jesus-Prometheus and Jesus-One-of-the-Boys.

Then there is the Jesus to fit the social liberationists of the twentieth century of all varieties: the Jesus-Bleeding Lord, Jesus, the Mystic, Jesus-Black, Jesus-Femina, Jesus-Gay, Jesus Christ Superstar, Jesus, the Revolutionist (*Jesus Now*, pp. 44-73).

Homo ludens

For us Westerners one image of Christ almost totally unknown is that of *Jesus Ludens,* a playful, joyful Jesus. The reason is that we have lost the joyfulness of childlike play and leisure. We live so much in the head. We are the little people in Jonathan Swift's caricature with spindly legs holding up a skinny body with an oversized head that continually topples us over. We need to contemplate the joyful Jesus of the gospels to refashion ourselves into his image and recover for us modern people the lost art of playful joy.

Play is always engaged in with joy. It creates an original space on the border of reality that opens us up to creativity of God working mysteriously when we learn to let go of our rational control over reality. In order to allow the true child of God, that unique person you and I are, different from God and from every other creature, to be birthed into being, we must learn to let go, a prime characteristic found in joyful playfulness. It seemingly is a leaving of the order imposed by science in order to enter into a larger aspect of integration and harmony of ourselves with all other created beings and with the Creator. Play is a time of leisure to complement the unique *thisness* in the created beings we encounter. It is important to be totally immersed in these moments so as to discover the mystery of God as the source of all life inside of the particular, joyfully creating new and exciting possibilities.

In play we learn to let go of our rational control of a given situation. It is reflected also in our attitude toward our habitual view of life, as we learn to give up patterns of static fixity that have been developed by our false *ego.* This means an openness in a process of continued transformation from fixity to new life and new creative forces within us, and in this concrete, important moment not to *do* or *conquer* or *gain* but to surrender to the mystery of greater being.

An *ego* orientated toward rational goals will always be concerned with ideas of how our lives really ought to be lived, rather than learning to open outward to new and exciting possibilities and let things happen, as children delight in living fully in this playful moment. The desire to "do" closes us from the desire to "become" more uniquely a child of God before him in new creativity.

The words from the Book of Proverbs capture something of this joyful playfulness of God's word in creativity:

> When he established the heavens I was there. . . .
> Then was I beside him as his craftsman,
>   and I was his delight day by day,
> Playing before him all the while,
>   playing on the surface of his earth;
>   and I found delight in the sons of men.
>
> (Proverbs 8:27-31)

Resistance to play in the West

When we in the West engage in play, we usually show a resistance to the true purpose of play, and we usually don't find any joy in such activity. I believe this is true because play is the medium through which the make-believe is brought into being and acquires the status of a reality that is closed to the rationally controlled mind. Such resistance is due to our Western culture's denial of any ultimate status of validity or truth given to the imaginary, the poetic.

Children at play teach us how to return to what Mircea Eliade calls *in illo tempore*, to the sources *of being* in an experience that uses more of imagination and heart language to touch God beyond any limitations imposed by our reasoning powers or by laws of science. Such reality is like a woman who desperately runs away from one who wishes to conquer her by force but who surrenders herself to the one who gently waits upon her free consent.

Return to the anima

We in the West are sensing the need of rediscovering the feminine polarity in our psychic make-up, that which Carl Jung defined as "diffused awareness," as opposed to the "animus" in us of "focused consciousness." Science has given us technology through the inductive and deductive rational systems. We have entered into outer space travel that has brought human life to the moon. With our advanced methods in medicine and agriculture we have the means of extending human life and feeding millions in the third world, of making this a more human planet for all world citizens.

Yet the pollution that comes as the price to be paid for such industry, the wars, the rampant social injustices, poverty and starvation, that not only still exist but are ever increasing, have forced us to go back into our past to find the forgotten feminine corrective. We need to recapture the poetry and play, joy and gentleness of our childhood. We need to be receptive to the mysterious in love that can be experienced only by self-emptying love in humble service toward the other.

We cry out in our society and in our Christian Churches for a God who is more powerful. We seek one who is also gentle, loving, joyful and suffering. Our Christianity is demanding that not only we individuals become integrated, healed and made whole persons but that the Jesus we worship and preach to others becomes also, as the gospel truly portrays him to be, a fully integrated person, one of love and joy.

Jesus joyful

Jesus was joyful and invites us to live lives full of joy by imitating his joy. His joy was founded upon being open and receptive to the work of the heavenly Father in his life. His joy was his way of existing in the truth of his Father's awesome transcendence in his life. The Father was greater than Jesus, and without the Father the Son incarnate could do nothing (Jn 5:30; 14:28). Everything Jesus had, by way of revealed word or power of healing and miracles, came to him from the Father (Jn 5:20).

The Father was always working in Jesus' life (Jn 5:17), and Jesus joyfully played and worked before him and with him, delighting the Father but also being full of delight. Jesus was not an automaton without free will, but in all things he turned inwardly to find his Father at the center of his being (Jn 14:11). There in the depths of his heart, his innermost consciousness, Jesus touched the holy. He breathed, smiled, laughed and cried in that holy presence of his infinitely loving Father. All outside created beings, touching Jesus in new, surprising experiences, were received by that delicate, sensitive gentleness in him as gifts. Absent were the moods of an angry, aggressive autonomy and uncontrolled self-indulgence. Jesus was always present to the Father, because the Father was always speaking his loving word in him.

The beautiful words of the poet, Gerard Manley Hopkins, describe the constant attitude of Jesus-Gift toward his Father, the Giver:

> Thee God I come from,
>   To Thee I go.
> All day long I like fountain flow,
>   From Thy hand out,
> Swayed about
>   Mote-like
> In Thy mighty glow.

All things holy

Wrapped in God's loving presence, Jesus was joyful, as he received his being from the Father and sought always to return himself completely to the Father in self-surrender. To do the will of the Father was his great delight. He joyfully met each person and each event with the excitement of a child discovering new reflections of beauty of his Father but also reflections of his own inner beauty as the child of so loving a Father.

The many references in the gospels to nature, to the inanimate and plant and animal worlds around Jesus, tell us of his joyful openness to the fullness of life in all of God's creations and his cooperation in "working with him" (Jn 5:17). Lambs freshly born, seeds sown in the soft earth, the rain and its cleansing power, the birds that never stored grain into barns, the fox in its den, the grape vines being pruned, the flaming sunset, spangling the west with portents of fair weather, all creatures shouted out to the gentle Jesus that his Father was near, holy and good, beautiful and loving. All this filled him with deep joy.

The words of the Greek novelist Nikos Kazantzakis express something of the joyful discovery by Jesus of the Father in his creatures:

> I said to the almond tree: "Speak to me of God,"
> And the almond tree blossomed.

> (*The Fratricides*, frontispiece)

Jesus found joy in playing with the children and blessing them "for it is to such as these that the kingdom of God belongs" (Mk 20:14).

Joy in his friends

Jesus surely found great joy, as you and I do, in his relationships with his friends. Some few, beyond the crowds that sought Jesus out for healings and miracles, Jesus allowed to experience his loving heart as ready to share himself with them in deep intimacies of words and silences, looks and touches. What joy he must have given to his mother, Mary, but he also must have received from her! If mothers exert a tremendous influence, far greater than human fathers, in shaping the attitudes and character strengths of their children, is it far-fetched to believe that Jesus learned the secret of finding joy in the ordinary events of daily, simple living from his mother? At Bethlehem and at Nazareth, during the infancy and early childhood of Jesus, Mary poured a heart of total love toward him as she lived out her *fiat:* "Behold, I am the handmaid of the Lord. May it be done to me according to your word" (Lk 1:38).

Jesus found joy in the uniqueness of each of the twelve disciples: "As the Father has loved me, so I have loved you" (Jn 15:9). He shared himself intimately for three years of his public ministry day and night. Even in their weaknesses as in their strengths, Jesus rejoiced in their basic goodness and manifestations of his infinitely beautiful Father. His tears at the tomb of Lazarus attest to how much joy his friendship with him must have brought Jesus. He loved Lazarus' two sisters, Mary and Martha, as his intimate friends. He ate at their table, and Mary seemed to have a special sensitivity and joy that must have brought a similar joy to the heart of Jesus.

Jesus discovered great joy in bringing the lost sheep home to his heavenly Father. If he could say: "Rejoice with me, because I have found my lost sheep," surely he must have found joy in accepting the repentance of Mary Magdalene, Zacchaeus, the repented Peter and all the other sinners to whom he brought the mercy of the forgiving Father. He was called a friend of tax collectors and prostitutes by his enemies. Not only does he seek out the repentant sinners and fill them with his joy and peace, but he does it often in an engaging, even playful manner, spiced with a sense of humor as, for example, when he conversed with the Samaritan woman at the well of Jacob (Jn 4:4-42). Who can fail to see his playful smile, as he looks up into the sycamore tree to call Zacchaeus down to receive salvation! He smiled at the enthusiastic conversion of his publican host: "Behold, half of my possessions, Lord, I shall give to the poor, and if I have extorted anything from anyone I shall repay it four times over" (Lk 19:8).

Jesus human

We can learn to bring joy into our lives, as Jesus in his humanity experienced the presence and sanctifying action of the Holy Spirit in every facet of his humanity. If Paul could appeal to the Corinthians' inner dignity because their bodies were holy (1 Co 6:19), how much more was this a living experience of joy for Jesus in his human body? Jesus not only found the Father working in nature all around him, in the fields, the sea, the sky, the changes of the seasons, the variety of plant and animal life, but also he continually discovered the Father in his own body, indwelling and working.

Seeing his Father in the materiality of his body as well as that of the world around him, Jesus enjoyed a joyful serenity and contentment in simply being there with the Father. Sin sets up a physical and spiritual nervousness in us, because we fail to see the loving presence of God in those relationships. We tend to exploit bodily gifts, as we see in our abuses of our basic appetites for food, drink, sex, material and intellectual possessions, honors and, in a word, pride of life, that destroys the possibility of lasting joy and brings only meaninglessness to our lives.

The Spirit in Jesus allowed him to grow "in wisdom and age and favor before God and man" (Lk 2:52). All anxiety was removed from his openness to meet his loving Father in each fresh moment. The situation was not objectivized as either holy or profane for Jesus. But from the inner presence of the Spirit he moved freely and joyfully through life's events and circumstances to respond fully according to the Father's will. His life, made up of each moment and his free choices within that moment, brought him into a growing experience that in all things he was the eternal child, only begotten, of the heavenly Father. Free from sin and self-seeking, Jesus was free to be loved infinitely by his Father and to strive to respond joyfully in a return of that love.

Jesus found joy in becoming more fully human in all moments of his earthly life, even in suffering and death, as he surrendered to his Father's working in his life. With joyful exuberance he could embrace all created beings and use them properly according to his Father's mind. His joy in encountering the Father in each of his creations was founded on an inner austerity in all of his human relationships and his use of the created. His mother, disciples, friends, food, drink, human pleasures were not his ultimate concern. He did not merely use them as instruments to glorify the Father, but they were *diaphanous* points to find the Father in the human context and to return love to him by serving each human person encountered.

Joy in poverty

Jesus discovered joy in his living a life very simple and basically poor. He lived poorly only because he lived by the inner richness of his Father's continued gift of himself to him in each created being he touched. It is the poverty that can be called *humility* that is at the basis of the joy of Jesus. Jesus was nothing; the Father was all. He is meek and humble of heart (Mt 11:29). He lives to surrender himself to do whatever the Father asks him to do, even unto death, and he does so with joy. Ultimately, Jesus shows his holiness and joy in poverty by being detached and unpossessive from the praises given to him by others. For this reason Paul could write: "For you know the gracious act of our Lord Jesus Christ, that for your sake he became poor although he was rich, so that by his poverty you might become rich" (2 Co 8:9).

Joy in service

Jesus came to serve, because service is love in action, and he was acting out in human ways the love of God the Father for his children. He, who was one with God in glory, emptied himself and became a suffering servant, even unto the death on the cross (Ph 2:6 ff). He who was master washed the feet of his disciples (Jn 13:1-16). He burned with an inner fire to actualize the presence of the Father in the lives of all human beings he met. "I have come to set the earth on fire, and how I wish it were already blazing!" (Lk 12:49).

He finds joy in living to remove from human lives any pain or suffering and replace it with exuberant, rich, happy, healthy and fulfilled lives. His service is love enacted, and love always brings forth joy in the one loving.

Joy in prayer

Jesus was consistently joyful, even in suffering, because he prayed not as a "doing" but as a living state of being always humble in total loving surrender and in complete worship to the Father. The evangelists grasped the intrinsic relation of Jesus' prayer and his joyful living always in the presence of his Father. The prayer of Jesus is tied intrinsically with the coming of God's kingdom.

Jesus usually prays in solitude (Mt 14:22), away from even his disciples, deeply immersed for long periods, even all night (Mk 1:35; Lk 6:12). He seeks the face of his Father in praise and thanksgiving, in petitions that follow from his desire that God's kingdom come. In prayer Jesus touches the holiness or self-sharing of the Father with the Son and all his human children and is filled with joy through his own holiness that lives only to serve the Father.

The priestly prayer of Jesus

It is when Jesus reaches the end of his earthly mission and is about to die freely as victim offered freely by himself, the high priest, on the cross that we see the depths of his joy, which he wishes to share with his disciples down through the ages. John's gospel records his priestly prayer that reveals the heart of Jesus present at the last supper. He establishes the new covenant in his blood, the goal of his earthly ministry. He looks also to his agony and to the cross in order that through his suffering and death he may share his joy with all his followers. "I have told you this so that my joy might be in you, and your joy might be complete" (Jn 15:11). His disciples, as he himself, would weep at his death, but their sorrow, as that of Jesus, would be turned into joy (Jn 16:20). "I will see you again, and your hearts will rejoice, and no one will take your joy away from you" (Jn 16:22).

In this prayer Jesus prays for his disciples, for their work in bringing about the kingdom of God, for the Church that would be built up in faith through their preaching of his teaching. Here we see

Jesus going forth in his suffering and death but with a joy that comes from his turning completely toward his Father in heroic self-emptying on behalf of sinners to fulfill the will of the Father and make it possible that we, even in our modern times, can still share in the joy of being the Father's children through the death and resurrection of his Son.

Joyful death

Only pinioned on the cross and dying slowly does Jesus become in human form the image of the unseen God who loves us with a perfect, dying love. On the cross the hour of Jesus has arrived. Becoming God's communicating Word of love in the *kenosis* of total emptiness, Jesus is overcome with the Father's love. His Holy Spirit comes upon him and inundates him with his fruit of love and exceedingly great joy. "Eloi . . . Eloi . . . My God, why have you deserted me?" (Ps 22:1; Mk 15:34).

At this moment the Father of Jesus, who had always been a blazing light of joy, bathing him with his smiling love, now seems clouded in fierce darkness. Now it is as though the Father's wrath is poured out against him. Jesus must feel the quagmire of the world's sinful filth suck him down and cover him with darkness. He has taken upon himself our sins. And by his wounds we will be able to be healed (Is 53:5)!

As Jesus surrenders completely to his Father's will, soft rays of light wove toward the darkness, just as the first sign of dawn with its velvet touch dissolves the darkness. In a seeming abandonment, Jesus gropes to look again upon the countenance of the Father he adored with such profound joy. He now experiences the paradox he had preached to others but in the most profound joy and comforting love of the Father's Spirit: "Blessed are they who mourn, for they will be comforted" (Mt 5:4). His sorrow turns into ecstatic joy, death is conquered and transformed into new life.

Before such infinite love of God the Father, Son and Holy Spirit, made manifest in Christ Jesus, suffering and freely dying on our behalf, our response must be a similar return of love by the power of Jesus' Spirit in us. We too can be empowered to suffer greatly, even unto death, and yet rejoice for the joyful Savior, risen from the dead, lives within us and is our joy and fulfillment of all our desires. "Because of this, God greatly exalted him and bestowed on him the name that is above every name . . . and every tongue confess that Jesus Christ is Lord, to the glory of God the Father" (Ph 2:9, 11).

Jesus, the Joy of Our Desires

We have contemplated Jesus in his humanity, as he grew in wisdom and knowledge and grace before God and human beings (Lk 2:52). But he also grew in greater love and joy, as he learned in each situation of his human existence to surrender totally to the Father. Now we wish to point out the main reasons why Jesus Christ, as divine and human, as the Son of the heavenly Father and also born of Mary, is the reason why we Christians can truly rejoice always in all circumstances in our earthly life, and he will be the joy of all our desires in the life to come.

It is through God's Word and Sacrament, Jesus Christ, that God most fully reveals himself and allows us to share in his trinitarian joy. We have no way of receiving God's love for us except through receiving the personalized love of Jesus Christ. "As the Father loves me, so I love you" (Jn 15:9).

If God is love in essence, then he is always seeking by his nature to share his being with us by communicating his presence to us. God creates the whole world as good, as a sign of his burning desire to give himself in faithful communion through his Word. In the Word made flesh, Jesus Christ, we can come not only to know God's very nature, but we can be brought into a loving communion with God's very being through the risen Lord's Spirit.

One main reason why most Christians do not live consistently lives of joy is that for them this sublime truth of the intimate indwelling presence of Jesus in each of us remains only an intellectual idea that all too often never quite makes it into the practical living experience of each moment of our daily existence. If we could learn to live in this inner reality of God's infinite love, always intimately outpouring itself through Jesus, the way, the truth and the life (Jn

40

14:6), what dignity and beauty and consistent joy would be called
forth in all our daily relationships with God and our neighbor!

Our human dignity

We human beings, of all God's creations, possess an intrinsic
relationship to the triune community. By possessing an intellect and
will, we are able in freedom to posit ourselves, each of us, as an *I*,
dependent on the absolute *I* of God. But sin has entered to disrupt
this harmony between God's communing Word and ourselves. We
have closed our spiritual ears of conscience to God's Word. We no
longer want to be present in obedience to his Word that speaks only
words of dynamic, unifying love.

The first step in realizing our potential as truly human beings in
vital, conscious communication and communion with God is to be
like virgin earth. Then God's Word would fall gently upon the
softness of our hearts and take root there.

We no longer are in intimate and loving communication with
God's Word. Through sin, we began our long pilgrimage in exile
and still live in alienation and deafness to God's Word within us. We
are absent to the community of God's personalized love of Father,
Son and Spirit. We are not present, therefore, to our true logos or
inner form that fashions us into a unique, beautiful person as God's
manifestation of participated beauty in us as we live in oneness with
God's creative Logos.

Yet God is continually speaking to our logos through his Word.
God is present, touching us in millions of ways, yet we fail to hear
his Word speak to us and effect a loving communication toward an
intimate communion between ourselves and the Trinity.

Responding to God's Word

The power of Christianity consists in us Christians believing and
responding to the living Word made flesh, Jesus Christ, who died,

rose from the dead and in the glory of the resurrection can now release God's Holy Spirit. We can be truly new creations in Christ (2 Co 5:17) and dead to the old creation, as we Christians live in the immanence of the risen Lord, Jesus Christ, who abides within us with his Father and Spirit. He makes it possible now for us to live a life that will never die. We need fear no one, for the very power of the Trinity dwells and operates from within us and through us in the world around us.

A Logos mysticism

The early Eastern Fathers, especially Maximus the Confessor (+662), following the writings of John the evangelist, help us to find joy in living according to the Logos in whom all things are created and have their true being (Jn 1:1-2). The whole world is inter-related in its harmony, according to the differentiated logoi, the created existences of individual creation according to the mind of God. All things are created through the Logos through whom the creative will of the Father flows into material creation.

The logos in each being is the principle of existence which relates a given creature to God as its cause. It also denotes the created existence of a creature founded in God's will that it should have existence. It is the principle of a coming-to-be and implies a continued participation in God's being. These logoi are outside of time, existing in the mind of God and contained in God's Logos, the second person of the Trinity, who is the first principle and final end of all creatures. These logoi in the mind of God are not inert models but the very creative power of God realizing itself in creation.

Here we see a very dynamic vision of a world united in the mind of God, of a world of ideal logoi in process of being attained, as the existential logoi in created beings move to completion under the power of the Logos, Jesus Christ, with our human cooperation. Sub-human creatures have to exist according to their God-given logoi. They have no free choice. A mountain cannot be turned into a river by choice. An apple tree cannot be by free choice a peach tree.

But you and I are each of us called by God to be a unique logos in vital relationship with God's Logos, Jesus Christ. This is a dynamic process of *synergism,* or working together with the vital and loving presence of the risen Lord living within us and communicating his Word to us.

A joyful listening to God's Word

We need a general emptying of our own driving, aggressive attacks upon God, others and the world around us and a putting on of a gentle spirit to listen to God, as he communicates himself to us through the risen Word incarnate, Jesus Christ. Thomas Merton describes this general emptying "that waits to realize the fullness of the message of God within its own apparent void. The true contemplative . . . remains empty because he knows that he can never expect or anticipate the word that will transform his darkness into light" (*Contemplative Prayer,* p. 112).

We discover inner joy as God reveals himself through his Word as found in holy scripture. This requires a listening on the levels of body, soul and spirit as God's Logos or Word comes to us as history, an intellectual message to us. Then God's Spirit reveals to us a fuller meaning of the Logos relating to our unique logos in loving oneness with Jesus risen, as we receive a special healing word of love in the broken time and space in which we listen to this Word. The Spirit also releases the dynamic power of God that gives deeper faith and hope in God's will to fulfill what Jesus' Spirit of love reveals.

We joyfully approach listening to the word of God in scripture with humility and gratitude but, above all, with childlike faith that God's Word made flesh is still with us unto the end of the world in his revealed word (Mt 28:20). Yet, it is always a fresh new word being given to us, as we listen with complete inner attentiveness and in deep faith, hope and love. Joy abounds in our heart, as we connect our logos, our unique, true self in Christ, the divine Logos.

Such listening means that we are also listening to God in his revelation within the Church in its authority to teach and preach God's word from scripture and from the living traditions of the historical Church.

Listening to God in other persons

A special listening to God's Word as an unfolding of God's loving presence is developed, as we learn to listen to God in others. This is the basis for developing more joy in every encounter with other human persons. At first we listen on the bodily level to God's Word speaking to us through others. We seek to praise God in the positive qualities found in those we encounter. We seek to move away from the negative qualities of the individual to move in each encounter from the bodily level into a faith, hope and love vision that will allow us to pierce beyond the evident negative side of the person to see deeper the Word of God and to listen to what message of beauty and love the Word is speaking from within the unique logos of that person.

This will require on your part a respect for the uniqueness of each person whom you meet and for the freedom of that person to be real. Love for others will be engendered with a corresponding joy only if you can trust in the basic goodness and inner beauty of others.

The greater our awareness informed by the Holy Spirit's wisdom we have of the indwelling presence of the Trinity in the deepest center of our being, the greater we will become conscious of this same divine, loving presence, surrounding and penetrating all other things. Gone are the anxious, aggressive moods to dominate each situation to satisfy our physical and psychic needs. A new global sense of God's presence is discovered in each human encounter, as we push aside the veils of the externals to enter into the inner, loving presence of God.

As we become freed from our false *ego*, the screaming lies and suspicious doubts about our own identity and that of others, we can remain humble and loving, gently looking into the eyes of each person encountered to see there the face of God, shining through as love in the unique gift of the other person.

Growth in conscious awareness of the indwelling Trinity

As you move continually away from yourself as the center of your value system, you move in a continued "conversion" toward the indwelling Trinity as your sole center. Such a movement in listening to God's presence from within you through Jesus Christ risen and his Holy Spirit admits of certain peak or threshold experiences. Jan Ruysbroeck, the fourteenth century Flemish mystic, teaches that the first level of breakthrough toward deeper interiority consists in the spiritual growth in the belief that the Trinity dwells within you and that, as often as you turn within and believe, you can expect to find God dwelling within you and loving you infinitely as a triune community.

At times this spiritual awareness, as an infusion of deeper faith, hope and love from God, quite unexpectedly comes upon you. It might be as you watch the ocean in storm or in peace, on a mountain top overlooking a beautiful sinking sunset in the west, in a moment of intimate prayer in your bedroom or during a retreat. The suddenness of the experience shows that it is a gift from God that quickens you to a new level of joyful awareness of the allness of God in your life.

The most important activity on your part is that, as often as you can, you have a free, spontaneous turning of your will to put on the mind of Jesus Christ who dwells within you and speaks God's word to you through his Spirit of love. You develop an *atunement* to listen to the same Trinity speaking through the Word of God through his Spirit in the very events of your daily life. As the Trinity brings you into a sense of your belonging through Jesus Christ to the very family of the Trinity, this brings you into a sense of unity with Christ and also a new appreciation of your very uniqueness as a beautiful person for whom Jesus has freely died but now lives to bring you into increasing levels of happiness in discovering your true self in him.

You know through this deep, abiding experience that you are being constantly loved by the three divine persons. You know yourself as an *I*, loved by three persons, each a *Thou*, in a *We* community of love. Now you are able to give yourself to others through the Word that has been spoken within your heart. This is the basis for your continued growth in inner joy that flows outward toward others. You go into the broken, sordid, filthy world around you, but you listen deeper to what the same Word that speaks you into your being is saying in this or that moment and event.

A trusting love

Everything that is happening around you is God gifting of himself to you and the persons around you. You may be slighted, insulted, rejected, even hated by others. Still, you stand firm and listen with an inner ear of trusting love. You know not only from whom you have come but also from whom all things are coming and toward whom all things are moving as to their ultimate goal.

You give up your mercurial, changing moods, attitudes and prejudices according to the whims and opinions of those around you. Yet you are humbly open as a loving servant to serve the deepest happiness of others. The *event* is being dynamically presented to you; from it God's Word can be brought to new birth by our free cooperation. By faith you can believe that Jesus is coming out of this moment in a new reflection of glory. What is happening now is that God is speaking and you are listening. You go into this event to discover inside it what has already been potentially stored there. You enter into the given event to find the Trinity coming out of it (*evenire* in Latin), and in that moment there takes place the loving union of your will and that of Christ, as you and he become ever more one.

"Speak, Lord, your servant is listening" (1 S 3:10), is your constant outpouring of love in humble, joyful service to be used by the Trinity, Father, Son and Holy Spirit to bring forth new life in others. You learn to yield gently to God's loving presence in yourself, so you can think and act as a whole, healed person. Aggressiveness against others disappears, as you joyfully allow the presence of the Trinity to come forth from within you through Jesus and his Spirit. From the depths of this given moment you encounter those around you in loving service. To listen and to surrender to the indwelling Christ in true love is the first step to true joy, and then loving actions follow.

Jesus—source of our joy

We have seen that true joy is not something we can bring about. The first and most enduring fundamental condition for deep human joy is that we live in harmony with Jesus Christ according to whose image or form we have been created (Gn 1:26-27). At creation the Trinity wrapped itself in love around our mother, the cosmos, and filled her with the seed of God. The child of that marriage of God and matter was Christ the Lord. With him in the joy of conversion we dance face to face, so close we breathe the same air, the Holy Spirit.

In this shared life God rejoices at seeing our uniqueness, our form in the form of his Word made flesh, Jesus Christ, who contains all other forms willed by the Father from all eternity. We also experience a sharing in God's divinity, as we find our true selves by looking into God's face and reflecting the glory of his Son in our own shared radiance given by God's Spirit. With Paul we can say: "There is only one Christ; he is everything, and he is in everything" (Col 3:11).

We find true joy only in discovering our unique, true selves as children of God, sons and daughters of the Most High, brothers and sisters of the only begotten Son of God, Jesus Christ. Through a constant conversion or change of heart, we can become new by the love of God. That love is poured out into our hearts by the Holy Spirit (Rm 5:5). We pass over from darkness into light, from our false *ego* to our true self, from our aloneness to a oneness with Christ. As the seed roots and grows into the tree of life, so in darkness of our anxious fears we send out limbs that twine with the arms of God around the world.

Attaining harmony in Christ

Jesus alone, therefore, can bring us into true joy, because he alone can bring us into "consonance," to use the term of Adrian van Kaam, meaning to *sound harmoniously together*. We find joy only when we receive this as a gift of the Holy Spirit, who fashions us into our unique person, loved by God through Jesus, the perfect image or form of the Trinity's love for us expressed in human form.

Only he can bring us full integration of body, soul and spirit in union with himself through his Spirit, whom he gives us in order to experience God's perfect love for each of us in Jesus Christ, who dies to prove that love.

That joy can be his gift to us, as he transforms our alienation and disharmony into ever increasing wholeness and harmony of our true imageness in his image. Our strength is in Jesus Christ, who alone can heal and save us from our false selves and lead us into the true persons we were meant to be in him. "He is the sacrifice that takes our sins away, and not only ours, but the whole world's" (1 Jn 2:2).

Contemplating the indwelling presence

The continued source of your joy is Jesus' indwelling presence within you, in the depths of your heart. This is what makes it possible now for you to be always present to him and him to you. No one can ever separate you from him, as Paul writes:

> For I am convinced that neither death, nor life, nor angels, nor principalities, nor present things, nor future things, nor powers, nor heights, nor depth, nor any other creature will be able to separate us from the love of God in Christ Jesus our Lord. (Rm 8:38-39)

Joy is yours, not only in your intimate union with the risen Lord Jesus, but also deep joy is yours in discovering the same indwelling light of Christ and his resurrectional presence shining "diaphanously" throughout the entire material creation, to quote Teilhard de Chardin's term. You are able to contemplate the physical world around you in the light of Christ's resurrectional power that raises up all things to a new sharing in his divine life.

You are given new eyes of faith, hope and love to see God's grandeur bursting forth in the words of Gerard Manley Hopkins: "The world is charged with the grandeur of God. It will flame out, like shining from shook foil." A grain of wheat, the sunset in the west, bursting through splintering clouds with its ball of fire, the innocent smile of a baby, the wisdom of an old man sharing his experiences of the godly in his life on a park bench. All things cry out to you that God is here. This place is indeed holy! With eyes of a child filled with wonder and joy, you open to God's living revelation in all things. You believe nothing can keep out the loving, inside presence of God as love in all things. As you act on that living faith, it becomes a reality. More and more, every moment with all your material involvements allows you to become more and more united with the inside, indwelling presence of God, the triune community of *I-Thou* in a *We,* of self-giving persons.

The joy of entering into the conscious awareness of what you will experience for all eternity in the condition called heaven is already yours, as you live as a child of your heavenly Father, one with Christ, his only begotten Son in his Spirit. But you also live joyfully one with your sisters and brothers of the entire human race and one with every material sub-human creature made by God for his glory.

Remaining chapters will describe more in detail how Jesus brings us into added dimensions of joy. It is fitting to conclude this chapter on Jesus, the joy of all our desires, with Paul's exhortation to find our joy always in Christ, who alone makes this possible both in this life and in the next to come:

Rejoice in the Lord always.
I shall say it again: rejoice!
Your kindness should be known to all.
The Lord is near.
Have no anxiety at all,
but in everything
by prayer and petition,
with thanksgiving,
make your requests known to God.
Then the peace of God
that surpasses all understanding
will guard your hearts and minds
in Christ Jesus.

(Philippians 4:4-7)

Tears of Joy

We stand on the mountain top and look into the face of God, reflected in all his beauties of created nature. Our eyes scan the horizon, and wherever they stop, we see the beauty of God breaking in upon us in the fluffy clouds, the pine trees cloaking the mountain side with a covering of fresh green, the rushing mountain torrents eagerly seeking the peaceful union with the ocean, the birds that take wing and soar toward their heavenly Father who feeds them and gives them cause to sing joyfully.

It becomes so easy for us to praise God in his infinite beauty in all his created beings. We stretch out our hands to touch, grasp, possess him, but our hands close into a nothingness as the *Unpossessable* escapes our weak clasp. We cry out from the depths of our soul to possess him more and more. Tears of joy well up from the depths of our heart. We weep to see how far God is still distanced from us.

Still we know with the prophets of old that the closer we approach God in his created beauties, the more aware we become of the arid sterility within our own heart. We see the scattered, dried bones strewn over the haunting memories of bitter joys of yesterday and of what could have been. As we look upon the mountain of God's grandeur, we see the valley of our own nothingness. We turn within and experience in the tomb of our inner darkness the light of God's tender love bursting upon us, ever so softly and healingly, and tears well up from the depths of our being:

> Have mercy on me, O God, in your goodness;
>   in the greatness of your compassion wipe
>   out my offense.

Thoroughly wash me from my guilt
   and of my sin cleanse me. . . .
My sacrifice, O God, is a contrite spirit,
   a heart contrite and humbled, O God,
   you will not spurn.

                                        (Psalm 51:3-4, 19)

A cry for healing

As we become more and more aware of the need within us for
inner healing, we cry out all the more in a constant plea that God will
touch us with his healing love. We "groan in travail" (Rm 8:22), as
we see our fragmentation. We feel caught in a prison of darkness,
and yet we see a delicate ray of light leading us out through the crack
of a *metanoia,* a conversion from the depths of being unto the Lord.
We hear the hopeful words of God whispered gently within the
depths of our soul:

Return to me with your whole heart,
with fasting, and weeping, and mourning.
Rend your hearts, not your garments,
   and return to the Lord, your God.
For gracious and merciful is he,
   slow to anger, rich in kindness,
and relenting in punishment.

                                        (Joel 2:12-13)

Daily we experience deeply within ourselves what Paul so vividly
experienced within his own being. Caught before the power of evil
like an inner cancer gnawing at our vital organs, we, too, with Paul
cry out for God's power to heal us of our "unspiritual" self. We feel
the same inner principle warring within our members. We find
ourselves helplessly doing that which we know we should not do:

But I see in my members another principle at war with the law of my mind, taking me captive to the law of sin that dwells in my members. Miserable one that I am! Who will deliver me from this mortal body? Thanks be to God through Jesus Christ our Lord. (Rm 7:23-25)

Desert Fathers

One of the great graces that I have received through my contact with the early Eastern Christian writers, especially the Desert Fathers, is the utter conviction of the necessity of recognizing our sinful condition, and in a state of constant conversion or turning of oneself totally to God as the source of all our strength, to cry out continually for his healing and transformation of such brokenness. This accent is summarized succinctly by the statement of Abbot Pimen, a fourth century Desert Father of Egypt: "Weep; there is no other way to perfection."

We Christians of the West all too readily think of one of the principal elements of prayer, that of sorrow and contrition for sins, as an attitude we seek to put on in preparing for the rite of reconciliation or in times of a retreat or during the annual period of Lent. We above all do not connect such inner sorrow for our sins with joy and, therefore, fail to experience what Jesus promised in the beatitude: "Blessed are they who mourn, for they will be comforted" (Mt 5:4).

When we begin to live more consciously and more interiorly, we make contact with what Paul describes as "the law of sin that dwells in my members" (Rm 7:23). Sin becomes something more than our deliberate acts of transgression against a divine law. We can learn much from the early Eastern Christians of the desert who had passed beyond the extrinsic aspects of the law and had entered into a deep self-knowledge of the inner movements of the "heart" as well as a deep consciousness of God's very immediate and tender love for them. In a word, sin for them was anything that would be an obstacle to joyfully living the good news of the paschal mystery.

Penthos: inner weeping

One central idea strongly stressed in the Christian East is that of purification and *penthos,* or the continued state of inner compunction of heart. In the West when we speak about sorrow for sins, purification and the constant thought of our sins, we regard this as totally negative. I believe the reason for this is that we have lost the concept of our littleness of heart, the conviction we should have of our absolute need for God's mercy and healing love. This conviction comes to us through the realization of our true, ontological position in regard to God.

It is evident throughout all the Eastern Fathers' writings that the first step in the spiritual life is always to put ourselves before God as we really are, which is in a state of poverty of spirit at our nothingness. But at the same time we remember the sheer gift we are because of God's humble desire to share his own divine life with us (2 Pt 1:4). We are nothingness of ourselves before his allness, and so it is only natural that Christian spirituality is based on this polarity: the *transcendence* of God and our own *littleness.*

Strangely enough, far from breeding in us any sadness or long-faced remorse or introspection, the realization of our nothingness before God is what gives us true Christian joy. Indeed, it fills us with great, childlike confidence in God's infinite love and providential care for us.

Have mercy on me, a sinner

As we sit within the inner desert of our hearts, as the desert Christians did in earlier centuries, we too learn to yield to the indwelling of Jesus Christ, the Divine Physician, who alone can bring life to us in greater and greater abundance. We cry out as often as we can, day and night, with distrust in our own powers to save ourselves but with childlike trust in Jesus the healer: "Lord, Jesus Christ, Son of God, have mercy on me, a sinner!" This demands a life of reflection, of sensitive inner knowledge in the light of the Trinity's indwelling presence and infinite love for each of us as unique children of so loving a God. In his light we see our darkness!

In that darkness we honestly recognize our guilt and sinfulness. We claim it as our own without justification or rationalization. We are broken and we need God's mercy. We are sinners and have gone astray. The spirit of compunction or abiding sorrow (*penthos*) for our godless past and the fear of a future without God strangely enough allows us in humility to contact God. God gives himself to the weak, the poor, the humble of heart, the needy. He looks upon the lowliness of his children who have entered into an experiential knowledge given by the Holy Spirit of their creaturehood.

This is the spirit found in all Christian liturgies, as the faithful bring a broken world through their own individual fragmentation before the merciful God to ask for inner healing of all that is false, proud and not loving. This is a vital part of our individual prayer before God. It is this that determines the depth of our true and effective conversion to the Lord.

There cannot be any true conversion, which is a turning toward God as the only center of our value system, unless there is a breaking of our pride and self-centeredness. This is the first step of a conversion, and it shows us that the Christian life is a constant conversion or a turning away from the false world of our own creation. Thus we can see why one of the elements in all authentic Christian prayer is a recognition of the inauthenticity which is guiding our lives. This is the sorrow and repentance that should be a part of all true Christian prayer.

The baptism of tears

As long as we modern beings continue to live unreflectively and superficially, we will not feel the urgent need to cry out in tears and in a constant yearning for repentance. Jesus Christ hears the prayers and cries of the little ones, the "poor in spirit" (Mt 5:1). For did he not himself promise that we would be blessed and filled with joyous comfort from him if we would mourn for our sinfulness and hope in his forgiving love? Jesus continually releases his Holy Spirit into our hearts if we are humble and broken in spirit.

The Holy Spirit purifies the penitent soul and fills it with a new enlightenment. We begin to understand in a new way our relationship with God and the world around us. Tears, at least interior weeping, are like a new baptism in the Holy Spirit. They make good the Master's words: "No one can enter the kingdom of God without being born of water and Spirit" (Jn 3:5). The Spirit convinces us of our own unworthiness to be loved by God, to be a favored child of so loving a Father. The deeper is our sorrow through the Spirit's illumination, the more the tears of compunction flow freely.

Like Job we too cry out: "My friends it is who wrong me; before God my eyes drop tears" (Jb 16:20). John Climacus gives us the common teaching of the desert mystics:

> Greater than baptism itself is the fountain of tears after baptism, even though it is somewhat audacious to say so. For baptism is the washing away of evils that were in us before, but sins committed after baptism are washed away by tears. We have defiled the baptism received in infancy, but we cleanse it anew with tears. And if God in his love for mankind had not given us tears, few indeed and hard to find would be those in the state of grace. (*The Ladder of Divine Ascent*, p. 114)

Weeping for others

As we move closer to the indwelling divine persons within us, we are filled with a deep shame for being such prodigal children of so loving a Father. In experiencing somewhat a reconciliation with the loving, forgiving Father, we remember our brothers and sisters around the world who still live far away from the Father's love, "eating the husks of swine" (Lk 15:16). We cry day and night, like Moses, with outstretched hands:

Pardon, then, the wickedness of this people in keeping with your great kindness, even as you have forgiven them from Egypt until now. (Nm 14:19)

We begin to experience that in many circumstances our love toward our neighbor is exercised in our silent weeping over the hardness of our relatives, friends, countrymen, fellow human beings. We begin to understand the anguish of the heart of Jesus, looking over Jerusalem and weeping:

Jerusalem, Jerusalem, you who kill the prophets and stone those sent to you, how many times I yearned to gather your children together, as a hen gathers her young under her wings, but you were unwilling! (Mt 23:37)

As Jesus the Good Shepherd would go up into the mountains to seek the one lost sheep, so we find ourselves praying, fasting and pouring out tears as we stand before God to ask mercy for others who do not know his loving mercy. "Let my eyes stream with tears day and night, without rest, over the great destruction which overwhelms the virgin daughter of my people, over her incurable wound" (Jer 14:17).

Effects of tears

As we seek to remain in a state of weeping before the Lord, begging pardon for our own sins and those of others, we discover several effects that flow out of such weeping. One of the greatest is the extinguishing within our heart of passions that formerly would burn us with desires which would destroy the love of God in our souls. We put to death now any inordinate desire as we surrender totally to the will of God. The hardness of our heart yields through a repentant spirit to a docility of listening and a promptitude to do whatever God commands. Basically it is humility that reigns in such

a purified soul, the humility of the Virgin Mary before God's wish
that she serve him as the mother of the Savior.

But the greatest effect of such inner weeping is that the Holy Spirit
fills us with his fruit of love, joy, peace (Ga 5:22). From the depths
of our heart there flows out a radiating joy, that even influences the
body with a newfound health, happiness and cheerful countenance.
And why should we not feel such a joy? Did not Jesus promise such
joy to us, his disciples (Mt 5:4)?

An unruffled calm is given to the repentant Christian with an
accompanied joy that no person or event can take from him or her.
For Jesus Christ has become Lord and Savior of such a Christian's
life. Such purity of heart allows us to see God in the sacrament of
each moment which fills us with joy, because now all creatures
proclaim the presence and love of God for us. "Then you shall be
radiant at what you see, your heart shall throb and overflow, for the
riches of the sea shall be brought to you" (Is 60:5).

Weeping begets joy

A strange alchemy exists between the sorrow for sins and the joy
that flows from the realized experience of being transfigured into
Jesus Christ through humble recognition of our inner poverty of
spirit. It is the Holy Spirit who quickens us to a deep realization of
what it means to be a divinized child of the heavenly Father through
the Son in the Spirit of love. It is a joy similar to the joy Jesus
experienced, as he learned to weep for the sin of the world and to
beg his Father's forgiveness for the ignorance of humankind.

In the Franciscan church of San Damiano in Assisi, there is a
beautifully carved crucifix which, like most popular and ancient
pieces of religious art, had a legend about how it was made. The story
tells of a pious Franciscan brother who started to carve out of a piece
of wood a crucifix to honor the suffering Savior. After the corpus
was finished, he became very perplexed as to how to depict the
suffering face of Jesus. He turned to the Lord in prayer but soon fell

asleep. When he awoke, he found the crucifix finished, no doubt by the hand of an angel!

What is unique about this crucifix is the combined expressions on the carved face of Jesus. When one looks up at the crucifix from one's right, the observer sees tightly drawn lines showing a man in the throes of tremendous suffering. His left eye is taut and fixed in a stare of empty agony. But if you were to move full center, you would see the lines elongated somewhat, giving the overall impression of a man dying in great peace. But, moving to your left, you would see the lines artistically lengthened, a curl of a smile on the side of the lips; in general a picture of radiant, youthful joy.

We Christians know that our transfiguration into Jesus Christ comes only through a dying process. It is the Holy Spirit who purifies us by enlightening us to experience our sinfulness and how much darkness dwells within us, how much sickness and alienation there are still to be healed by the merciful love of Jesus the Savior.

This same Holy Spirit gives us a second baptism unto water, but this time the water comes from our interior weeping through an abiding sense of sorrow and shame before the awesome, loving God-Father. Weeping cleanses us from passions and attachments to ourselves as the center of our existence. It allows us in great, burning desire to live only for God. Joy is the paradoxical result of our inner weeping. As we stand day and night in intercessory prayer for the salvation of the world through Jesus Christ, our sorrow turns to joy through the unshakable hope that the Spirit breathes into us constantly.

Holy Mary Full of Joy

Jesus is the image of the Father, and according to this image we have all been created (Gn 1:26). Yet, God's holiness in Jesus is still too awesome. He is still God and rejoicing in the eternal joy that exists forever between the Father and the Son in the Holy Spirit. God gives us human beings a human sign, an image that has come into existence as a human person born as we, totally human, not divine by nature as Jesus. Mary is the image and sign of what God has destined us human beings to become in Christ Jesus.

At the beginning of his restoration of the human race to its original grandeur and dignity that Adam and Eve had lost by sin, God raised up Mary as the sign of perfect human holiness to which we are all called in Jesus Christ. Yet she, like us, was in need of the redeeming grace of the only mediator, Jesus Christ. "Because she belongs to the offspring of Adam, she is one with all human beings in their need for salvation," as the Second Vatican Council decreed (*Lumen Gentium,* Part II, 53).

Mary is God's preview, as it were, of what we human beings by God's grace can hope to become. She comes as the first Christian, the first human being who is totally conscious that Jesus Christ lives in her, and she surrenders totally in faith and loving obedience to serve him. She is the beginning of the Church, as an individual member or the collectivity of individuals in whom Christ's Spirit dwells and operates to produce fruits of love, peace and joy, the signs of the Church in the world. She is in a miniature form what the whole Church will become by God's divinizing grace.

Karl Rahner compares the difference between the graces of holiness that Mary received and our own gifts:

Mary does not differ from us because she possessed these gifts. It is her possession of them from the beginning, and incomparably, that is the sole difference between her and us. As for the content of this gift, its nature and intrinsic meaning, the eternal Father could not intend anything for the mother of his incarnate Son, without intending it for us too, and giving it to us in the sacrament of justification. (*Mary, Mother of the Lord*, p. 49)

It is Mary's holiness, ultimately, that helps us believe and hope that, as Mary through the Holy Spirit was always in Christ, so we since our baptism have been in him and are growing by our daily cooperation with his love and grace to approach her union with Christ. Mary in popular Christian devotion is the Star of the Sea. Her spiritual perfection shines like a beacon to all of us, as we battle the darkness of the sea and its sudden tempestuous storms to move ever closer to the goal of our life. We are called to reach her holiness and her joy. By God's grace she is what God wants all of us to become.

Joy and holiness: a growth process

Mary's life illustrates for us that we can never separate her joy or our own joy from her continuous and thereby our own growth in holiness. She is a model for our growth in joy and holiness as always inter-related.

For her holiness and her joy consist in a process of discovering that God's love has truly surrounded and completely penetrated her. She had to push her consciousness, always by the power of the Holy Spirit, to new levels of awareness that God was her allness and she was mere emptiness without God. She was being filled by God's continued gift of love. In her poverty and humility, Mary gradually grew in surrendering adoration that was actualized by her fidelity to do at all times God's holy will in her regard. She was filled with the holy fear and reverence for Yahweh's awesome presence. Yet she knew his sweetness as the source of her abounding joy.

Not only the holiness of the Old Testament was known to Mary in her prayerful study of God's word, but she became that holiness by a continued experience of greater intensity. Mary's holiness unfolded in the context of her daily life, and so did her joy increase in the same process. She became full of grace by yielding herself to the promptings of God's Spirit. Like us, she too had to cooperate with God's grace at each moment of her life.

Characteristics of Mary's joyful holiness

By reflecting on the picture we find of Mary in scripture and guided by tradition, especially in popular and liturgical piety, we can draw out some of the appealing elements of Mary's joy and holiness.

One characteristic of Mary's holiness is summed up in the simple word: *contentment. Contentment* is the opposite of a physical, psychical and spiritual nervousness. Such restless nervousness usually flows from a faulty relationship between ourselves and God.

Mary enjoyed from earliest childhood a contentment that was a result of the Holy Spirit's gifts of deep, abiding faith, trust and love toward God. She knew she was guided in all events of her life by the powerful hands of a loving God-Father. She was moved by the Spirit to experience God as Abba, Father (Rm 8:16; Gal 4:6). She was content with each moment, for her heavenly Father was continually manifesting himself in the present "now."

> We know that all things work for good for those who love God, who are called according to his purpose. For those he foreknew he also predestined to be conformed to the image of his Son, so that he might be the first-born among many brothers. And those he predestined he also called; and those he called he also justified; and those he justified he also glorified. (Rm 8:28-30)

Before her divine Son had preached about the loving care of the heavenly Father (Mt 6:26-30; Lk 12:22-31), Mary experienced the peace and joy that came from living a life of constant abandonment in loving trust to the heavenly Father. The Greek Fathers called this childlikeness *parrhesia,* not one virtue but a way of life, a state of being before the Father that flows from the new nature that the Holy Spirit works in the heart of the baptized Christian. Mary enjoyed such a trusting confidence in each event of her life.

Paul could have been describing not only his own but also Mary's attitude toward life's situations when he wrote:

> For I have learned in whatever situation I find myself to be self-sufficient. I know indeed how to live in humble circumstances; I know also how to live with abundance. In every circumstance and in all things I have learned the secret of being well fed and of going hungry, of living in abundance and of being in need. I have the strength for everything through him who empowers me. (Ph 4:11-13)

Filled with joy in all things

Mary learned to trust in Yahweh and to live in his joy and peace. "Commit your fate to Yahweh, trust in him and he will act" (Ps 37:3-5). She was filled with joy, and for all things she gave thanks to God (1 Thes 5:18). She was the happiest of all human beings, for her strength was completely in God her Savior. She felt his sustaining power upholding her in her poverty, as the eagle's pinions hold up the weak eaglet that seeks to fly only under the supporting strength of the mother eagle (Dt 32:11).

Mary's joy was not dependent upon the circumstances in which she found herself. Whether she was seeking in distress her lost Son in Jerusalem or scorned by those who mocked her crucified Son on Calvary, Mary remained always "content," always filled with a deep, abiding joy, because her strength was in her God. Happiness can be a fleeting thing, often depending on many ephemeral factors. We do not need to feel happy to be content, but no one, not even

Mary, has ever been content without being joyful. She teaches us not
to run from the situation that brings us suffering but to find contentment with that situation, because God is the sole strength.

The Father is always working in each event

Her contentment was built upon her faith vision of God working
in all events of her life. "My Father is at work until now, so I am at
work" (Jn 5:17). This developed in her a profound trusting hope.
Hope recognizes in Mary her own weakness. It places all her strength
in God's goodness and holiness. Hope in God for Mary produced a
reverence that allowed God perfect freedom to do with his servant
Mary whatever he wanted. Mary's hope makes her wait for God's
richness to be poured into her emptiness whenever and wherever he
wishes. God is all, and Mary knows that alone she is nothing. But
her poverty before God is her true riches. "For he has looked upon
his handmaid's lowliness. . . . The Mighty One has done great things
for me. . . . He has shown might with his arm . . . but lifted up the
lowly. The hungry he has filled with good things" (Lk 1:48-53).
Mary was content and filled with joy at all times, because in her
littleness, in her truthful stance before the greatness of God, she
continually experienced that "whoever humbles himself will be
exalted" (Mt 23:12). God turns away from the proud, but he gives
his grace to those who are humble (Js 4:6). God delights in Mary,
because she is authentically what he wants all human beings to be.
This brings consonance and harmony into her life and into our lives
too, if we are humble before God as she was.

Mary most human

As we have already pointed out, Mary evolved into holiness
through the human situations in which she discovered the providential love of the heavenly Father working. We are left with no details
of her childhood or her growth up to the annunciation. We can only

imagine what she must have experienced, as she found herself falling in love with young Joseph. His strong body, supple, yet tender, gave to her a "holy" revelation of God unobtainable in any other way. She found God's love in his pure love and self-sacrifice for her.

We too are to grow in sanctity and increased joy in human relationships, since God is always perfecting his love for us when we love one another (1 Jn 4:12). Mary opened herself to the inner beauty of God's loving presence in her love toward each person to whom she related. She came alive and discovered God inside each human encounter. Her faith made her joyfully alive and discovered God in each person, as she found him within herself always working as she worked with him. Thus she was able to find God's loving presence everywhere. Her trust allowed her to give herself to the human situation without fear or nervousness. God's Spirit of love allowed her to be delicately open and sensitive to the needs of others.

Pure of heart

Her joy flowed out of her purity of heart. "Happy the pure in heart; they shall see God" (Mt 5:8). This earth has never seen a vessel as pure as Mary. We can say that we will never see a more "human" person than Mary. She saw reality as closely as God sees it. God infused into her a purified vision that permitted Mary to see the "insideness" of God's presence. She reverenced that presence and humbly strove to serve God's will in each circumstance. "Behold I am the handmaid of the Lord. May it be done to me according to your word" (Lk 1:38).

Our devotion to Mary has stressed in times past her purity. What the Holy Spirit is moving us to appreciate in Mary is her humanness, her growth in faith that necessitated vital contacts with a material world, with real women, men and children that have bodies and passions, moods and depressions. As she gave herself to God in each person, her knowledge and understanding and wisdom of God, of herself and of humankind grew. Nazareth was important to Mary's growth in contemplation. Each person in that village allowed her to meet God in him or her and thus opened Mary to meet God in all human beings. This was the basis for her ever-increasing in joy in the human context.

We cannot imagine that Mary traveled much beyond Galilee and Judea within the confines of Palestine. She surely did not give herself to great crowds of people of disparate needs and backgrounds. But her growth in humanness and joyful holiness was determined by her freedom to be opened totally to the God-presence in each human encounter. Mary's holiness and joy were not developed by running away from the material world or in spite of it but precisely in that diaphanous, material world that presented to her purified gaze God at the heart of matter.

The freedom of Mary

Mary was, to use Paul's analogy, Sarah, the free woman, the sign of the heavenly Jerusalem, in contrast to Hagar, the slave woman, the sign of the Jewish nation enslaved by law. Entering into an ever-deepening awareness that she was a child of the heavenly Father through the power of the Holy Spirit that overshadowed her constantly freed Mary to be the freest human being this world will ever see. For she at all times strove not to fulfill merely the law but to be the servant of the Lord. She shows us that Christian freedom is an ongoing gift to us by the Holy Spirit. Freedom is to obey God, to take our whole life in hand and dispose it totally in loving service to God. True freedom is not concerned so much with choosing good over evil as with determining ourselves in all choices according to the good pleasure of God.

Mary, by the Spirit, knew her nature was such that the imperative to obey God was freedom to act as her total nature dictated. Freedom for her was to be the person God destined her to be. "Now the Lord is the Spirit, and where the Spirit of the Lord is, there is freedom" (2 Co 3:18). The Spirit within her gave her a new, inner law that freed her from any formalized extrinsicism. She experienced a continued joy through a freedom that the Spirit gave her in a continued growth process that was first rooted in his gift of faith. She responded in faith to the love of God by her complete surrender to serve him in all things.

Her faith led her holiness to a strong hope that with God all things are possible. God could do whatever he wished with her. She would hope for a greater fulfillment of God's glory even though she already had experienced a great share in that glory.

But her joy and holiness have to be measured and described in terms of love, that in Mary grew out of the Spirit's faith and hope operating within her at each moment of her life. Mary had the freedom to love, and true love, self-sacrificing love on behalf of others, always brings forth true joy that no one can take away. She freely placed herself in service to God's Word, an inner presence of God's love incarnated and living in her. As she received in prayer experiences God's love calling her to participate in returning love, Mary became progressively more free to love others by seeking to serve them with the greatest joy.

She experienced always the paradox, that to be free is to become a slave to serve others in love. She knew that she was called to serve others in love, as she thrilled to love herself as the emptied receptacle to be filled with God's goodness.

> For you were called for freedom. But do not use this freedom as an opportunity for the flesh; rather, serve one another through love. For the whole law is fulfilled in one statement, namely, "You shall love your neighbor as you love yourself" (Ga 5:13-14).

Mary is holy and full of grace and joy, because God filled her with his Spirit of love, and because she freely cooperated with his grace at all times. We are privileged by that same Spirit to recognize that her holiness and joyful living are normative for all of us. If Mary is so holy and joyful by God's grace and her continued cooperation, why not also we?

A Joyous Humility

We have been called by God to live "in spirit and in truth." Jesus promised that "if you remain in my word, you will truly be my disciples, and you will know the truth, and the truth will set you free" (Jn 8:31-32). Yet, we all too clearly see that we are not free but are slaves who live constantly lives full of lies. Our self-centeredness and pride convince us that we can live independently of God. We refuse to believe that only God is God and from him we have received all we have and all we are, except our own sins. We lie to each other as we inflate our accomplishments and possessions to exalt ourselves in ego-worship.

And thus we continue to put on masks and play roles before each other, hollow persons who speak in hollow voices, stuffed with the straw of ego, our bones too dry to live. Anxieties and fears increase as we continue to be false to those true selves that might rise like living water from God within us, from the true source of being out of which we sprang, if we only would die to our selfish pride.

What was originally meant by God to have been a world both unending in its richness and diversity and a harmonious whole, unified by love, has been distorted into a world seen darkly through the glass of separation and alienation. In the mythopoetic account in the book of Genesis, we are shown how Adam and Eve disobeyed God, taking power into their own hands. A life of self-inflicted pain, of joyless selfishness, of brother killing self and brother and sister, of human beings killing nature around them in the name of conquest, is the result of that original sin. "Cursed be the ground because of you! In toil shall you eat its yield all the days of your life. . . . By the sweat of your face shall you get bread to eat" (Gn 3:17, 19).

God's children have grown up in a single moment and know what they have done. Their punishment is the very thing they thought they wanted—to be alone with themselves, separated from God. The disobedient children engendered the adults. The pages of the Old Testament, filled with Towers of Babel, harlotries of the heart, violence between brother and brother, nation and nation, dramatically cry out to us that this is our unhappy story also. Adam and Eve's sin is ours and our fig leaf excuses are no different from theirs!

The effects of pride

We live in a false world that we continually create within ourselves and show on the movie screen of our own minds. No one except us comes to this interior theater, but we hardly notice, so in love are we with our own false image and its creator, ourselves. In every movie we play the hero, refusing to see that we are also the villain. We fear God's terrifying punishment, God's self-revelation, as utterly different from our poor selves, and so we hide, not behind fig leaves as did Adam and Eve in their nakedness, but behind the masks and games that separate us from God, from our once honest child-selves, and from the world around us.

Like all pathological liars, in the end we come to believe our own lies. In our "splendid isolation" we tell the world we are happy and healthy even as we drink, drug, and eat ourselves to death. We desperately seek to be loved by others rather than to love them, and we try to take their love by force. We destroy the very love we crave in the depths of our being, while our false selves feed on the flesh and bone of our brothers and sisters.

If we kill our brothers and sisters, they cannot love us, and without their love we cannot live. We must let our false selves die so that our brothers and sisters may live, and we with them. Yet we seek to place the blame on others for our misery in our unhappy pride, as Adam tried to convince the God of truth that he was no sinner, since the fault was that of the woman God gave him (Gn 3:12).

The hand that kills us is our own, as the hand that took the fruit was Adam's, but we refuse to accept the truth that we ourselves cause our own unhappiness. It is no wonder that God pitied and loved us broken, blinded children enough to die at our hands so that we might see God and live.

Paul had the courage to face his loneliness and helplessness, to be faithful to his true self. So he had the courage to confess:

> But I am carnal, sold into slavery to sin. What I do, I do not understand. For I do not do what I want, but I do what I hate. . . . Now if I do what I do not want, it is no longer I who do it, but sin that dwells in me. So, then, I discover the principle that when I want to do right, evil is at hand. . . . I see in my members another principle at war with the law of my mind, taking me captive to the law of sin that dwells in my members. Miserable one that I am! Who will deliver me from this mortal body? Thanks be to God through Jesus Christ our Lord. (Rm 7:14-24)

Made to be children of God

Although sin abounds in us, grace does more abound. Our bodies and souls are meant by God's eternal plan to be joined into a likeness of God's incarnate Word, Jesus Christ. We can become healed and made whole by God's grace in Christ Jesus and the Holy Spirit. We are our unique, true selves when we realize that we are truly children of God, sons and daughters of the Most High, and brothers and sisters of the only begotten Son of God, Jesus Christ.

Paul writes: "In him you also who have heard the word of truth, the gospel of your salvation, and have believed in him, were sealed with the promised Holy Spirit, which is the first installment of our inheritance toward redemption as God's possession, to the praise of his glory" (Eph 1:13-14). God overturns the values that guide us to choose what our false egos say we should choose. Money, power, aggression and separation are to be replaced by the defenseless love of Jesus.

God chose, especially in the suffering and death of his Son, to confound the proud of this world. "For God's foolishness is wiser than human wisdom, and God's weakness is stronger than human strength" (1 Co 1:22-25). God's wisdom, so different from the wisdom of this world, flows out gently through the overwhelming Spirit of love. It is the beginning of true love that begins to lead us into true humility, as we begin to share in the wisdom of the Trinity, Father, Son and Holy Spirit who know that the true self within their community of love and within all our love relationships has identity only when love becomes an emptying of oneself to live humbly for the other's happiness.

Perfect love casts out all fear

If God's love had not reached out ecstatically through Jesus Christ, we would have remained always in our self-centered pride since we would not have known how much God loved and wanted us to share in his love. We would, therefore, have held onto all our dark doubts and ancestral fears. Because God sees us each as unique and worthy individuals, God gives birth to us again in a new life, mothering our true self in Christ.

We could never have demanded such love from God. Yet, as though from some primeval knowledge, we hoped for this unconditional love. In answer to our longing, God longed for us. "I have loved thee with an everlasting love. My affection for thee is constant" (Jer 31:3). God showed us the divine image, God's very self, in Jesus. When we see Jesus broken and emptied on the cross, we truly see the Father in his love for each of us (Jn 14:9). Jesus mirrors God's love for us in his free gift of himself out of love. Hearing his words we hear the voice of God, who promises to gather all men and women as healed children, as they become one with Jesus in the gift of himself.

Jesus risen is always calling all of us to come to him and learn of him how to live in true love and joy.

Come to me, all you who labor and are burdened, and I will give you rest. Take my yoke upon you and learn from me, for I am meek and humble of heart; and you will find rest for yourselves. For my yoke is easy and my burden light. (Mt 11:28-30)

Since Jesus embodies all he teaches which he has received from his Father and he commands us with the very authority of the Father, we, his disciples, must study him, for he is the way, the truth and the life (Jn 14:6). The spiritual rest Jesus gives us comes not from our observance of any static, extrinsic laws but from assimilating and living Jesus' values and attitudes, indeed, to live in him, for without him as our strength we can do nothing (Jn 15:5) but to continue to be blinded by our pride. Such a yoking of ourselves to him becomes a light burden for his true disciples.

Thus Paul exhorts us Christian disciples of Jesus:

Have among yourselves the same attitude that is also yours
in Christ Jesus,
who, though he was in the form of God,
did not regard equality with God
something to be grasped.
Rather, he emptied himself,
taking the form of a slave,
coming in human likeness;
and found human in appearance,
he humbled himself,
becoming obedient to death,
even death on a cross.

(Philippians 2:5-8)

Humility: the basis of all virtues

Let us seek to explore this topic of humility that summarizes the values that Jesus lived by and which he asks us to live by if we are to discover our true self in our intimate union with him. Just as all our good works and virtues are meaningless if we are not primarily motivated by true love (1 Co 13:1-13), so also humility is the pre-condition and basic foundation for all authentic virtues.

This is true, because humility is the true and right relationship of ourselves to God, neighbor and all of creation. It has its essence and strength in the knowledge, given by the Holy Spirit through the gifts of faith, hope and love, that it is God who works in all created beings and that our true self finds its greatest dignity in yielding to him in perfect, childlike trust and abandonment in full consent to be obedient to his will and to do nothing independently of God as the complete source of all that exists.

James writes in his epistle: "God resists the proud but gives grace to the humble" (Jm 4:6). Pride is the irrational, ignorant, most primal root of all sin. It is primarily in its many forms the independence and glorification of the false self in a conscious or unconscious turning away from complete dependence on God, the giver of all good gifts. "All good giving and every perfect gift is from above, coming down from the Father of lights with whom there is no alteration or shadow caused by change. He willed to give us birth by the word of truth that we may be a kind of first fruits of his creatures" (Jn 1:17-18).

The infection of pride

Pride is always very close to our every thought, word and deed, ready to remove God as the ultimate source of all gifts, even of all we are or can accomplish. It exalts ourselves as the center of all our values. Pride brings into our lives a stubborn will to refuse to live according to the image and likeness of God which dignity he holds out to us as the basis for true harmony, joy and peace. Pride destroys our true freedom, which consists in choosing to take our lives and freely to determine to give ourselves as gift in return to God for his self-emptying gift of himself to us in Christ Jesus.

Humility on the other hand comes into our lives by the freeing power of the Holy Spirit who leads us out of slavery to sin, death and the law into true liberty as God's daughters and sons. The Christian under the Spirit of Jesus risen understands that slavery to egoism is destroyed by Jesus' great personal love for each of us individually. True freedom is now revealed as God's love in us, bringing us into a slavery now to belong totally to the heavenly Father through Jesus Christ and the Holy Spirit.

Humility: the basis of true Christian joy

We can now begin to see how humility is also the foundation of all true Christian joy. Joy follows from our living in humility, as Jesus lived on this earth and found joy in each moment of his life, as he put the heavenly Father as the center of all his human choices. He strove, as we must strive, to allow his Father to be all in his thoughts, words and deeds. Jesus ''humbled'' himself in obedience to the Father's will, and for this reason the Father raised him up and exalted him (Ph 2:6-13).

Jesus teaches us, as we have seen in a preceding chapter, that all joy and peace came to him because in his humility he freely surrendered himself with all his powers to allow the Father to work in his life (Jn 5:17). He was always joyful in his submission and dependence upon the Father's will. Because Jesus humbled himself to the Father, he found it possible also to humble himself as the suffering servant to all who came into his life, since he had "passed over" from any prideful self-exaltation.

Here we find the nature of true humility. Jesus teaches us that humility, and therefore true joy and peace, all flow from the Spirit's gift of love. And humility is love in active self-surrender to the Father to live fully by dying to any form of pride or self-centeredness.

Elements of true humility and source of true joy

Since humility and joy are so intimately connected, as a foundation is connected to an upper building, the elements that make up true Christian humility also make up true Christian joy. The first element in a joyful humility is the active awareness we must have of the omnipotent and omniscient, all loving and all good God as the primal Creator of all created beings and the goal toward whom all creation moves as toward its fulfillment. We must see that we come from God as rational creatures, called by God's free election (Eph 1:4-6) to share in his triune life.

All that we are and all that we receive comes to us through God's active, gratuitous, free choice. As creatures we are not the center of our *being,* but we owe all to God's free will. We receive all our being from God. He is the one who *is,* while we, in the words of Irenaeus of the second century, are "empty receptacles to be filled with God's goodness." We can only be "non-being" if we are separated from God's sharing of his being with us through his creative gifts. We understand the joyful and humble response implied in the words of Catherine of Siena: "That thou shalt be and I shall not be."

Worshipful adoration

This element of humility is the first and continued stage of the conversion of the prodigal son and daughter of the long-awaiting, forgiving Father. "I am unworthy to be called your child." Yet this is a joyous response to live in total surrender to God. It recognizes humbly one's nothingness and unworthiness in the light of a non-being life in which God was excluded as the center and source of all life and power. It, above all, reaches out in worshipful adoration toward a so forgiving and tenderly loving God.

Before, our prideful *ego* sovereignty defied and excluded God's supremacy in our value system. But now a reverence for God's greatness and perfection brings about a humble abandonment to live as Ignatius in his *Spiritual Exercises* writes: "*ad majorem Dei gloriam, for the greater glory of God.*" Such purity of heart and reverence are shown in a practical way according to Paul's exhortation: "So whether you eat or drink, or whatever you do, do everything for the glory of God" (1 Co 10:31).

Such humility dissolves all sadness and depression and brings about a joyful longing to live only for God, as habitual "bias" toward self is dissolved by God's love for us and replaced with God as the source and goal of every thought, word and deed.

Knowledge of self in the knowledge of God

Francis of Assisi gives us the second element of true humility and source of authentic Christian joy in his words: "Who art thou, and who am I." We encounter in God's awesome transcendence ourselves in both our sinfulness and weaknesses, our areas of brokenness deeply embedded within the labyrinthine layers of our unconscious. We humbly recognize that God is the source of our entire being, which brings about a new and personalized relationship between each of us as individuals with God as Trinity.

> Know that the Lord is God,
>   he made us, his we are;
>   his people, the flock he tends.

> (Psalm 100:3)

A strange alchemy occurs on the spiritual level of our relationships with the triune God. We become more intensely aware of our own inability to live as we ought by our own power. In our weakness we now learn to trust in God's burning love for each of us in our uniqueness. Our weaknesses now become our strength, as we place all our hope in Christ's love.

How dramatically Paul wrote about his "sting in the flesh" and how he prayed three times to Christ to heal him of his weakness. He learned from the risen Lord that the Lord's strength was sufficient for him, because God's power is made perfect in human weakness. Thus Paul gives us an application of the second element of true humility when he writes:

> I will rather boast most gladly of my weaknesses, in order that the power of Christ may dwell with me. Therefore, I am content with weaknesses, insults, hardships, persecutions and constraints, for the sake of Christ; for when I am weak, then I am strong. (2 Co 12:9-10)

Childlike abandonment to God

The third and most intense element of true humility is the degree of childlike abandonment we give to God in the present moment, as we trust in his infinite goodness and love for us to be our strength when we are weakest. How childlike is the statement of Therese of Lisieux that was at the basis of her "little way":

> Jesus has pleased to show me the one and only road that leads to the furnace of love. This is the abandonment of a little child that goes to sleep without fear in the arms of his Father.

Such childlike faith and trust are graceful gifts of God's personal presence to the broken, little ones of his kingdom. He condescends to come to their side to help them. He pledges his unconditional word that he will always be faithful. "Always true to his promises, Yahweh shows love in all he does" (Ps 145:13).

When we are given such a gift of God's presence as dynamically loving us in every event and moment, then complete abandonment is our true response to his fidelity. "With God on our side who can be against us?" (Rm 8:31). The Spirit allows us to let go of our preconceived ideas of reality, of what we deem to be important and not so important. He gives us a whole new set of values that are truly illogical to the worldly-minded (1 Co 1:18), that only the little children of the kingdom of heaven can understand (1 Co 2:10-12).

The third mode of humility

There is something unique in what Ignatius in his *Spiritual Exercises* terms the "third mode of humility." In the deepest fulfillment of humility it becomes a loving self-surrendering as a constant, prayerful response to the God-Man, Jesus Christ. The Holy Spirit binds us into a nuptial union with Christ Jesus. With Paul we can proclaim at all times and in all circumstances of life:

> I have been crucified with Christ; yet I live, no longer I, but Christ lives in me; insofar as I now live in the flesh, I live by faith in the Son of God who has loved me and given himself up for me. (Ga 2:19-20)

Ignatius wishes to lead the retreatant in the following of Christ to live aggressively as Jesus did, actually to choose, in order to be more like him, to live in a way that the Christian decreases while Jesus increases (Jn 3:30). Ignatius expresses the third mode of humility thus:

> The third degree is the most perfect humility; . . . supposing equal praise and glory to the Divine Majesty, the better to imitate Christ our Lord, and to become actually more like to him, I desire and choose rather poverty with Christ poor, than riches; contempt with Christ condemned, than honors; and I desire to be esteemed as useless and foolish for Christ's sake, who was first held to be such, than to be accounted wise and prudent in this world. (#167)

The folly of the cross

This is a wisdom that partakes of God's wisdom when he chose the folly of the cross for his Son to reveal the passionate, fiery love of the triune community for each of us. "We proclaim Christ crucified, a stumbling block to Jews and foolishness to Gentiles, but to those who are called, Jews and Greeks alike, Christ the power of God and the wisdom of God. For the foolishness of God is wiser than human wisdom, and the weakness of God is stronger than human strength" (1 Co 1:23-25).

This is the joyous humility of the saints that made suffering and persecutions a source of sweetness and a deeper oneness with Christ Jesus. It is the burning love of God that abounds within us through the Holy Spirit (Rm 5:5) that drives humble Christians deeper down into the abyss of their "nothingness" in order that God may be revealed in all his glory, "so that God may be all in all" (1 Co 15:28).

This is the authentic sign of joyous humility and the sign of the Christian having died to self-centeredness and already in this life to share in the resurrection of Jesus risen (Rm 6:10 ff). The Christian paradox of true love and humility is that the triune life, given to us in baptism, through a series of deaths as we empty ourselves, fills us with the utter fullness of God (Eph 3:19). The wisdom of God becomes our wisdom as we joyfully and aggressively live out Jesus' teaching and example: "For everyone who exalts himself will be humbled, but the one who humbles himself will be exalted" (Lk 14:11).

The exaltation and sharing in the glorious resurrection of Christ even now must never be viewed as a reward for the "humble" actions we perform. It is a sharing in the radiant transformation of Jesus by the inner Taboric light that shines within us by the indwelling Trinity. It cannot be done to our own power to acquire humility by the acts we do. We must deny to ourselves the falsehood of our own self-assertion as an act of independence from God's allness. But as we put to death the terrible lie of holding on to God's gift of life and claiming ourselves as the sole source, we discover with all the saints that death to selfishness brings life in God's triune indwelling and that humility is the test of how matured is our Christian joy in Jesus Christ. No new life without death to a lower, illusory holding on to our self-centeredness life, no true and lasting joy without true humility.

> For whoever wishes to save his life
>   will lose it,
> but whoever loses his life for my sake
>   will save it.

> (Luke 9:24)

Joy in Suffering

There are many things we can be "anti." We can be anti-war, anti-pollution, anti-poverty. But one thing a Christian cannot be is anti-spring. This would be equivalent to being anti-hope and anti-new life. Spring is the most basic perennial experience in our earthly experience of the beginning of new life. After a long, dull winter during which frost and snow have stripped nature of all signs of verdant life and covered each created thing with the kiss of cold death, spring comes with its clarion call of hope, which announces that what lay so many months in apparent death is about to stir unto new, fresh life.

In his poem, "An Ode to the Setting Sun," written near the end of his life, Francis Thompson summarizes the paradox that one form of seeming death prepares for a new level of fresh life. "There is nothing that lives but that something must die. There is nothing that dies but that something else will live." Jesus Christ taught this law many times in simple and often quite blunt language. Above all he lived this law which is nothing less than the universal law of love.

> Unless a grain of wheat falls to the ground and dies, it remains just a grain of wheat; but if it dies, it produces much fruit. Whoever loves his life loses it, and whoever hates his life in this world will preserve it for eternal life. (Jn 12:24-25)

When the seed seems most at the point of death, that germ of life bursts through the dead shell, pushing up through the earth a green sprout of fresh life. In paradoxical language Jesus insisted that if anyone wanted to be his disciple and obtain eternal life, he or she had to begin by a "dying" process. He or she had to enter into a suffering, but one that would bring joy in the very suffering, since such loving suffering would already be bringing forth new life.

81

We have to take the risk of surrendering ourselves to his guiding Spirit of love by giving up a lower level of existence which seemingly allows us to be in control, ruling our own life, to accept Christ's offer to move to a higher level of existence. Thus Jesus taught and lived this necessity for all of us, his disciples, to deny ourselves in our false non-being, to suffer in living to love God with our whole heart and to love ourselves and our neighbors in unselfish love, which is always a form of dying. But through the Spirit's faith, hope and love, we can suffer in truly loving which is always accompanied by joy (Mt 16:24-25; Mk 8:34-35; Lk 9:23-24).

Jesus lived death unto new life

Jesus lived out this law in his own earthly life. The gospel accounts of his life present it in terms of the *Exodus*. He was passing over from death unto life everlasting, a life he would be able to share with us human beings through the outpouring of the fullness of the Holy Spirit. The Greek Fathers were fond of calling the Savior of the world the *sperma logikon,* the logos seed of divine life that was inserted into our suffering and sinful humanity. The soldiers on Calvary lifted that divine seed aloft and then plunged it into the hole prepared for it in the earth.

Its whole side was split, and at the very moment that the Seed seemed to have perished, an inner life burst forth into a new and glorious, eternal life. Jesus was risen on Calvary in that momentless moment, as he passed over in loving surrender to the Father on our behalf. He was glorified by the Father in that moment that he cried out triumphantly and joyfully: "Father, into your hands I commend my spirit!" (Lk 23:46).

Suffering will be the lot of every human being. Whether we accept our sufferings or not, we will still have to bear a great deal. As Job found out, suffering will always remain a mystery to our puny reasoning powers. But Jesus Christ came, not to remove all suffering from us, nor to give us a definitive, rational answer why we human beings have to suffer so much and why God permits evil persons to continue to perpetrate evil, especially upon the innocent and helpless. He came to give to us, his disciples, himself as the *way*, the *truth* and the *life* (Jn 14:6) by opening up to us through the Spirit's faith, hope and love a vision and the strength through his indwelling, risen life to "suffer with him so that we may also be glorified with him" (Rm 8:17).

Kinds of suffering

Before we can present a Christian view of joy in suffering, let us see some of the main areas where all of us have already found sufferings and will no doubt continue to do so. We suffer passively in the mere act of growing from infancy to childhood, from being a youth to reaching the full maturity of adulthood. There are biological, psychological and spiritual sufferings that "happen" to us and are necessary if we are to grow more fully on the levels of body, soul and spirit relationships. As water seeks its own level, so in God's providence the crosses that come to us seek the level that can offer us the greatest good in growth of loving surrender to the centrality of God in our lives.

There will be the suffering of sickness, physically, psychicly and spiritually. There will be the bunglings of ourselves and of others acting upon us, the doubts, fears and anxieties from our own creatureliness and sinfulness to cope with the many problems of life. Ultimately there will be the greatest diminishment of death itself to lead us into the final, physical suffering in order to pass into eternal life.

There will be suffering on a more active level of working in the sweat of our brow for our daily bread. This will entail much discipline and above all much monotony. It calls for a usual, banal routine that in the ultimate analysis cuts away at our egoism, as we learn to transcend the momentarily monotonous in order to move into a larger vision of loving, creative labor.

There will be inner trials to resist impatience toward the failings of others around us, but, above all, in the area of faith to surrender to God's loving care in darkness of the soul and spirit where we seem to feel God's absence in a cloud of darkness. J. P. de Caussade, S.J., in his classic, *Self-Abandonment to Divine Providence,* writes:

> The life of faith is nothing else than a perpetual pursuit of God through everything that disguises, disfigures, destroys, and, if we may use the word, annihilates him.

It is in such interior suffering that we learn to surrender ourselves to the supremacy of God's perfect love and goodness, working in every event of our lives.

A Christian meaning to suffering with joy

We are not to seek answers from Jesus, the revealer of God's wisdom and love, who communicates to us through his humanity. The Word made flesh came to take upon himself all our sins and suffering. He suffered, as you and I do. He became one of us, not to be an answer to solve our problems about evil and suffering, but to become our *way,* whereby we could rise in a transformation from suffering with Christ to a sharing, even now, with him in glory (Rm 8:28).

From the gospels we can see how Jesus, in his personal encounter of himself with evil and the human suffering he had to endure from various sources, became gradually, in a process of struggling in faith, hope and love with such evil and suffering, transformed by the very darkness of the trials into the eternal, glorious light that he was from all eternity (Jn 1:5).

The reason Jesus could move to a higher dimension of viewing evil and suffering was that he was vitally conscious that everything he did came to him from his Father. He lived only to please him and bring him glory. Over and over, he confessed that he was nothing, while his Father was all (Jn 5:19, 30).

The secret of how he could suffer, even die, joyfully was that in the very trials and "crosses" he pushed himself to greater depths of consciousness of his ultimate worth and meaning as a unique human being who derives all meaningfulness from his complete dependence upon the Father. His primary motivation in every thought, word and deed is to serve the wishes of his heavenly Father. He lives in his loving presence, as he becomes more and more surrendering in each moment to the working of his Father out of love for him in his earthly life. As the Father loves him and serves him in all things, so Jesus loves and serves the Father by loving and serving us.

Love is suffering unto self-emptying

That service, in God's eternal plan, was to be pushed to such self-forgetting that Jesus would be brought to becoming a free gift of himself on behalf of the human race. He would literally and freely give himself to die for each of us. His attitude toward evil and suffering can never be separated from his consciousness that he was to become the perfect image in human form of how much the heavenly Father loves his children, even unto death.

Jesus' attitude before suffering and even death itself is seen as an act of faith, hope and love, as he is turned in complete submission and obedience to do his Father's will. He disregarded the shamefulness of the cross (Heb 12:2), enduring it for love of us.

As Jesus experienced in prayerful communion his Father's perfect love for him, he grew in his sensitivity to what love was asking by way of a self-oblation. He wished to go beyond the boundaries imposed by justice or even by the delicate whisperings of what the Father wished of him in any given moment. I like to call it "creative suffering." It is what brings joy to suffering and keeps love alive. It is fire touching dry wood and making it turn into fire also.

So likewise he makes possible through his Spirit that we too can accept suffering with joy by responding to the indwelling Trinity, Father, Son and Holy Spirit, in us and working in all events around us in childlike abandonment. We are graced to live in the mystery of faith in Jesus Christ as the image of the heavenly Father and to rise from what seems to be a disastrous, meaningless, even irrational suffering or failure to embrace a new oneness with the risen Lord Jesus and even now participate in his glory.

Interiorizing our faith

Faith is the midwife that assists us in emerging out of a dark cocoon of fear, doubt and ignorance as a newborn butterfly. Rather boring, monotonous events, even those of little or great suffering, can be consecrated by faith, hope and love into a *felix culpa,* a happy fault, leading from death to new levels of oneness with God and other human beings in love.

Such trying moments can become true participations in the resurrected life of Jesus. In the very moment of uniting our sufferings and consecrating them to God with Jesus out of love for God and fellow-human beings, we already enter into a new sharing in his glory (Rm 8:17). As we abandon ourselves in loving surrender, we experience a new insertion into the life of Christ.

Living in the heart

The first stage of increasing our faith and making it more "interiorized" by greater union with the risen Lord is, in the words of the early Fathers of the desert, "to push the mind down into the heart." It is to enter into the "inner closet" that Jesus spoke about when he instructed his disciples how to pray in his Spirit (Mt 6:6). This is a continued call to a conversion as we move away from our "carnal-mindedness" in order to enter into a transcendental presence to the indwelling Trinity.

It is the "place" of the heart wherein we are to meet the risen Jesus, who reveals through his Spirit's faith, hope and love that this suffering at hand can truly work unto good to those who love the

Lord (Rm 8:28). John of the Cross in his short work entitled *Counsels*, written as his advice to a lay brother or a clerical student, gives us a short synthesis of how we can live habitually in God's abiding presence in our heart. In order to allow Jesus and the Father and Spirit to hold complete supremacy in our lives and to bear joyfully all suffering and trials, he gives four areas of tasks and challenges in order that Jesus be the center of our lives.

These are: 1) resignation 2) mortification 3) the practice of virtues and 4) to seek bodily and spiritual solitude or aloneness with the Alone. To foster inner joy and peace and become grounded in God's allness, we must control in our "resignation" our curiosity and unkind judgments of others. We are to mortify our false selves by accepting the passive and active diminishments with inner patience and total dependence upon God. We are to practice all the virtues Christ exercised in his earthly life, summarized by the two great virtues of obedience to please solely God in all things and humbly to exalt others before ourselves. Finally, we are to allow our lives to be hidden in Christ Jesus (Col 3:3), as we contemplate in solitude the indwelling Trinity as the center of every thought, word and deed.

The second stage for interiorizing our faith that brings us into love with its accompanying joy and peace is to seek to know who we are in the very throes of suffering. Sufferings can force us as gifts from God to ask ourselves with urgency: "Who am I?" In seeking the answer we are forced in our brokenness and sinfulness, our "zeroness" of any power to bear with meaningfulness such seemingly illogical trials to confront who Jesus Christ really is for ourselves.

Praising God in all things

The sign of our emerging into a new level in Christ Jesus before our loving Father through their mutual Holy Spirit is our readiness to praise God with great joy in our hearts in all circumstances. We readily praise and thank God in prosperity when we joyfully receive from God health, riches, or, at least, all the temporal things we are in need of: honors, friends, successes in our undertakings.

But the true follower of Jesus learns through the Holy Spirit's infusion of faith, hope and love how to praise God in all seasons, under all circumstances. Praise is what flows from the depths of our joyful being as we surrender lovingly to God, who is in all things loving us and showering us with the gift of himself in whatever happens to us. We must believe by God's revelation, both in the Old and New Testaments, that God is love by nature. He always acts only out of love for us.

With Hannah, the mother of Samuel the prophet, we too can pray:

My heart exults in the Lord,
   my horn is exalted in my God.
I have swallowed up my enemies;
   I rejoice in my victory.
There is no Holy One like the Lord;
   there is no Rock like our God.

(1 Samuel 2:1-2)

With Job we can rise above our fears and agonizing suffering to exclaim: "Though he slay me, yet will I trust in him" (Jb 13:15). As Paul and Silas prayed and sang praises to God from prison (Ac 16:25), so we can raise our hands to God and pray: "We give thanks to God and the Father of our Lord Jesus Christ."

Our ability to rejoice and give praise to God in all prosperity and in all suffering depends on our childlike faith in God's great love for us. Adversities test and purify us as we praise God always solely because he is good and holy. Adversities allow us to humble ourselves before God, that he may raise us up to a new union of love with him through Jesus and his Spirit.

So humble yourselves under the mighty hand of God, that he may exalt you in due time. Cast all your worries upon him, because he cares for you. (1 P 5:6-7)

Suffering with Christ

At this moment in thousands of hospitals throughout the world or in homes there are people lying in beds with pain-racked bodies and staring wildly at ceilings and walls, looking for an answer to "Why this pain?" There are lepers, the crippled, the blind and the deaf, persons dying slowly from AIDS or cancer as their vital parts are eaten away. So many sick and suffering and all wondering: "Why this pain?"

Still sadder than any picture of human suffering is the realization that so much of this pain is wasted pain. People are forced to suffer and do not realize that their very suffering can be the occasion for their greater union with Jesus Christ. Perhaps most of us would have taken our places on that hill of Calvary when Jesus of Nazareth suffered and died on the cross. We possibly would have shaken our heads too in bewilderment and asked: "Why did he suffer this crucifixion? Why those nails through his hands and feet, why the crown of thorns, and the scourging? Why all these insults, spitting, and finally, the slow death? Why such a terrible loss?"

Filling up the suffering of Christ

Peter teaches us the necessity of our suffering, not because we have done wrong, but out of obedience to Christ's teachings. "Now who is going to harm you if you are enthusiastic for what is good? But even if you should suffer because of righteousness, blessed are you. Do not be afraid or terrified with fear of them, but sanctify Christ as Lord in your hearts" (1 P 3:13-15). If Jesus promised his disciples they would have to suffer persecutions for his name's sake, then it is important to understand the relationship of our suffering to Christ's suffering and our communion with him, our head and risen Lord, and with all members of the body of Christ.

Paul gives us a bold statement:

> Now I rejoice in my sufferings for your sake, and in my flesh
> I am filling up what is lacking in the afflictions of Christ on
> behalf of his body, which is the Church. . . . It is Christ in you,
> the hope for glory. It is he whom we proclaim, admonishing
> everyone and teaching everyone with all wisdom, that we may
> present everyone perfect in Christ. (Col 1:24-28)

We might ask ourselves: In what way can Paul and ourselves fill
up Christ's suffering? We must deny any implication that Christ's
suffering is incomplete and that we can complete what he failed to
do while he was on this earth.

Members of the body of Christ

If we keep in mind the analogy Paul uses of the Church as made
up, like the human body, of many members and each member
composed of cells that are interrelated with all other living cells of
the entire body, then we may be able to understand a higher motive
for accepting our suffering joyfully. We will avoid any "private,"
self-centered view of suffering and now only suffer joyfully with and
for Christ, that we might be in greater union with him. But we might
also suffer in loving service for other human beings, that they too
may experience the joyous union with Christ.

What brings us the intense joy that the martyrs and great saints
experienced as they lived in ecstatic oneness with Christ, the risen
Lord, is that we can become sharers in Christ's suffering. He makes
available to us, by having taken upon himself all our sins and
suffering, his suffering on the cross. Through faith in Christ's
passion we find redemption that is fresh and being applied to us
through his ever-present dying-rising existence as head of his members in his body, the Church. This is most perfectly symbolized in
the celebration of the divine liturgy and climaxed in the reception of
the eucharist.

Building the body of Christ by suffering love

If we manifest in time and space the suffering of Christ when we accept our suffering with joy in loving union with Christ risen, we also to that degree witness and aid in bringing the resurrection of Christ to fulfillment in his body, the Church. Suffering with joy, because we are in most intimate union with Christ and his suffering passion and resurrection, is the same as suffering to build up God's kingdom in this world. Here is the peak of how the paradox of our suffering can be accepted with intense joy.

It is not that we are to offer our pain as compassionate sufferings added to Christ's suffering. It is rather that we offer our suffering with more compassion, as we extend in our time and space the perfect, compassionate suffering of Jesus for all human beings. Our sufferings are now accepted with joy since we suffer as members of the body of Christ. He is our head. We suffer with him and in and for him to build up his body.

Such sufferings have a creative, eschatological effect for whatever trials we accept in loving care and active responsibility to lessen the suffering of other human beings. We believe this acceptance will help to bring about the future of the fulfilled Christ, the total Christ. In every moment of suffering out of love for others, we also share in raising the entire body of Christ to a higher level of loving union with Christ, the head.

As we are purified and live now only to glorify the Father through the suffering and merits of Jesus, his Son, we burn with zeal and joy to see his merits and his name, as we groan in the Spirit of Jesus on behalf of a race of people who know not the compassionate love of God for each of them in Jesus. As we experience the burning love of Jesus who has freely died for each of us, we will want to live lives of emptying of self and living for others in joyful service to the first person who enters our life.

God is calling us to let his suffering Word go among men and women to localize his loving, suffering presence in our present world. Loving, humble service, that brings always the possibility of creative suffering, especially as we seek to become the good Samaritan to the least and the most insignificant, the oppressed and the fearful, the lonely and the depraved, becomes a joyful desire that describes best the love of God which abounds within our hearts through the Spirit given us (Rm 5:5).

How can we say we love others if we are not ready to suffer with them, to take upon ourselves a sharing in their suffering? Yet when we realize that we are united with Christ risen who calls us to reconcile the broken, sinful world to God through his sufferings that are localized in time and place by the sufferings of us members of the head, then we can truly suffer with joy in all trials that come to us. With Paul we too can desire to be co-crucified with Christ, as we live no longer we ourselves, but it is the life of Christ who lives in us and suffers as head through us, his members.

How can we bring the healing love of the Savior, Jesus Christ, to the suffering whom we encounter, unless we have learned to suffer joyfully and meaningfully in Christ, the risen Lord? Only then will they experience Jesus as the Good Samaritan if we show an active compassion toward them because we have learned that the course of suffering in love leads to glory. What we do to the least in loving and joyful suffering we really do these things to Christ! This is how to live the paradox of suffering in joyfulness.

Walking in Joy
with the Angels and Saints

One of the most devastating human experiences is that of loneliness. This fact is true because God has created us out of the exploding love of the trinitarian community and placed into our hearts that constant drive to find our uniqueness in a human loving community during our earthly journey. We are to continue to find our uniqueness in and through such communities in the life to come when we will discover God, Father, Son and Holy Spirit, in and through such loving communities established on this earth.

But how often we have been so lonely that we have felt there was not a single human being on earth who loved us and truly cared for us. We longed for someone to understand, to listen and to give a bit of affirmation, and no one called or knocked on the door. We are all, from time to time, caught in such doldrums that we begin to doubt whether we will ever escape from such loneliness.

The communion of saints

What sadness and loneliness drive out all joy in our lives when we lose a loved one. Yet our Christian faith gives us certitude that those who depart from the confines of this world are fully alive in their new life. All the relationships, conscious thoughts and loving desires our loved ones had before death are still very much with them and even cry out for greater fulfillment.

But have we exercised an active faith in the truth that we can be in touch with our departed loved ones? And what joy could be ours at all times if we believed that we could walk in their presence and still rejoice in their love and other beautiful traits? And what joy would be ours also if we actively exercised a faith at all times that we can be in communion with all the human saints and angels who should be the source of much joy as we experience their loving service on our behalf!

Teaching of the Church

We do not need merely to "hope" that we can make contact in love with our departed loved ones as well as with the great saints and angels. It is a firmly established tradition in Christian teaching that all Christians form one body of Christ. ". . . One body and one Spirit, as you were also called to the one hope of your call; one Lord, one faith, one baptism; one God and Father of all, who is over all and through all and in all" (Eph 4:4-6). Christ, through his death and resurrection, has been constituted by his Father the head of this body.

This body knows no separation between the members and the head and among the members who are still on earth or are now enjoying the blessed life to come. This fellowship in Christ links all Christians together under Christ by the bonds of faith and the sacraments, especially baptism and the eucharist. We truly are parts of the whole and belong to each other (Rm 12:4). Each of us members of the body of Christ has a special role and special gifts or charisms to be used in loving service to each other to build up the body of Christ (1 Co 12:12-27). We lovingly belong to each other to the degree that we are consciously and lovingly obedient to Christ the head. "So we, though many, are one body in Christ and individually parts of one another" (Rm 12:5). The whole body is dependent on Christ for his life-giving Spirit of love. Yet each part is dependent upon the other, especially those closest to one another, in order to be nourished and strengthened.

Joyful help from the saints

Thus, as the doctrine of the Church as the mystical body of Christ developed in the early Church's teaching, so did the doctrine develop that the purified saints, who have died filled with the Spirit of the risen Jesus, were able to bring healing to others still on earth or those in need yet of healing in the state we call *purgatory.* Christ's power, especially his healing love, not only comes to persons on earth through the living saints, filled with deep faith, hope and love, but it continues to come to us and those already in eternal life through the intercession of the great Christians who are now with Christ in glory. Within the first five centuries of Christianity this doctrine of the communion of saints evolved. It is based on the solid belief that death does not separate the great saints, the apostles, martyrs, confessors, from those still living on earth or from those still undergoing healing therapy after death. This teaching, so ancient in the Church's doctrine and devotional life, assures us that all members who are in the body of Christ,whether on earth or in the life after death, remain joined not only to the head, Jesus Christ, but to each member.

I would like to highlight the joy that should be ours from this great truth, namely, that the great heroes, the saints and also the angels, continue to share in bringing the healing love of Jesus to all of us who are needy or broken. These "athletes of Christ" grow in greater love as they humbly and lovingly seek out those in need whom they may love through service. But this important doctrine of the communion of saints has great importance and should bring us much joy in our relationships with our own deceased loved ones.

They may not be as "great" as the great saints and angels venerated in Christian piety through centuries of devotion, but they are "bonded" to us personally with very special human ties of love. They have entered into purification before us. We see how we are needed to assure them of our love so that they can break down any unloving habits they may have formed in their earthly lives. But they can also help us in the process. Part of their purification-glorification or entrance into the fullness of "the maturity of Jesus Christ" means that they have need to exercise love and thus become a greater loving member in the body of Christ.

Need of us

This means that they need us in order to allow their love for God to unfold and be actualized in a new, expanded, conscious way. They reach out toward those with whom they have been united in love while they were on earth.

Let us first consider the great, glorified saints and angels and see how they can be the occasion for great joy as we still journey on this earth. Let us see how we can joyfully be in communication and in communion at all times with them as they seek to extend the healing love of Jesus to us through their powerful application of the one high priest, Jesus Christ, head of his body, the Church. And then we can reflect on the special joys that can come to us as we are in communion with our departed loved ones who can also help us in amazing ways.

Guardian angels

Part of the incarnationalism of Christianity is the constant belief held by the Church that God uses his creatures to manifest his perfections to his created children. Out of this basic truth there evolved the doctrine about angels as the emissaries of God's power and activated love brought into our lives. Rooted in the Old and New Testaments' doctrine about angels, the early Christian writers taught that angels are the channels, not exclusive, through whom God orders the course of this created world. Part of the work of the angels, therefore, is to help and protect God's children in order to lead them into the fullness of redemption and full citizenship in the heavenly kingdom.

Angels show their love for God through their service of other creatures, just as we are enjoined to show our love for God by serving one another. Augustine teaches that angels form the heavenly city of God and this segment of the holy city comes to the help of the other part that is still pilgrimaging below. Both parts one day will be united and even now are one in the bond of love (*Enchiridion,* 56).

Most of the Christian writers of both East and West taught clearly that each baptized person enjoys the protection and guidance of an individual angel. The Cappadocian Fathers, Basil, his brother Gregory of Nyssa, and John Chrysostom, clearly taught that those who believe in Christ and belong to the Church have their own individual guardian angels to protect them and to urge them on to good works.

We should rejoice, especially in those moments of great trials, doubts, fears and loneliness in the truth given to us by the Church that God ministers to us on earth and in the life to come through his angels and saints. Such "ministering spirits" (Heb 1:14) are found throughout holy scripture as the messengers of God or powers stemming from God. What is important, without our trying to dissect their spiritual nature, is that angels make God's goodness concrete, both in this life and in the life to come. From scripture and the writings of the early Fathers we discover angels as God's protection against dangers of spiritual evil powers. Basil taught that, as cities are protected by their ramparts against the attacks of enemies, so the Christian is protected by the guardian angel (*Homilies on the Psalms* 33, 5).

Source of help and joy

The teachings of the great writers of the Church hold out to us the help angels as instructors can give us, who lead us on to perform good works and who intercede for us who are placed in their charge. It is a gift from the teaching Church for us to believe that at our side is God's infinite power, unfolding through the ministry of a world of angelic spirits. In our present world where we are faced with so many perplexing forces of evil, belief in the ministering love of angels should not be a childish "cop-out" into a world of fairy-spirits, but it should be a grace from God, through belief in the teaching of the Church, that strengthens us in our struggle against such evil.

We can learn to communicate joyfully with God's communicating love by walking daily in the presence of our special guardian angel, who brings to concrete focus our belief in God's ever abiding and activating presence as love in all details of our lives.

Saints of God, intercede for us

We should enjoy also a special joy in our daily lives as we activate our faith in the powerful intercession of the saints who now live in glory. How natural is the Christian belief down through the centuries that the saints, so full of God's love, wish to continue to serve those in need, especially those of us on this earth. Origen, of the third century, in his treatise, *On Prayer,* developed this doctrine of the powerful intercession on our behalf. He shows that, if the virtues are practiced in this life for one's neighbor, they will be most perfectly exercised in heaven by the saints for those still on earth and for the departed still in need of healing.

He builds his argument on Paul's teaching: "So that there may be no division in the body, but that the parts may have the same concern for one another. If one part suffers, all the parts suffer with it; if one part is honored, all the parts share its joy" (1 Co 12:15-26). He believes that Paul's words: "Who is weak, and I am not weak? Who is led to sin, and I am not indignant?" (2 Co 11:29), can be applied also to the saints, who grieve and wish to do all they can to help the weak members in the body of Christ (*On Prayer* XI, 2, 1).

How natural is the belief of Christians down through the centuries, therefore, that the saints rival each other in holy competition to bring more of Christ into being in his body among the members of the Church militant and suffering? What a source of constant joy for us, as we believe that all the saints, Mary, the apostles, the great martyrs, confessors, virgins, not only desire to serve us in love to know Christ, as they know him in glory, but that in a way they need us, underdeveloped brothers and sisters, so they may exercise God's immense love burning within them by letting it out in loving service to us needy ones.

They need the sinful and ignorant who live in darkness and absence of their Lord and Savior in order to measure out as it has been measured out to them (Lk 6:38). Is it far fetched to believe that the saints, to the degree that they have died to themselves and allowed Christ to live in them, go out to all human beings, but in a special way to the most forlorn and needy, to suffer with them and to take upon themselves the burden of the weak? They see the Lord face to face, yet they go forth continuously to see the Lord's face in those who suffer, especially from ignorance and the pre-conditioning sins imposed upon them by inheritance and society. They are now growing in grace and glory, in oneness with Christ the head, as they bring healing love to the heavily burdened.

Personal joy in the saints

I personally have found much joy wherever I have been, in traveling or alone away from others, to bring myself into the presence of the saints, including those special heavenly friends, whom through grace and personality I have been drawn to in a special attraction and spiritual friendship. The saints see us as members of the body of Christ. They see what we could be, as they humbly see, not only what they were in their human frailty and even sinfulness, but what by God's grace they have become: divinized as children of God, one with Christ in glory.

Devotion to the saints is devotion to Christ, the head, who empowers his followers, especially those who are with him in glory. "All power in heaven and on earth has been given to me. Go, therefore, and make disciples of all nations, baptizing them in the name of the Father, and of the Son, and of the Holy Spirit. . . . And, behold, I am with you always, until the end of the age" (Mt 28:18-19).

Mary, pray for us sinners

We have already meditated on how Mary grew during her lifetime in joyful service to God and neighbor. In a very special way Mary shares her joy with us by her powerful intercession and living presence among us. Is it any wonder that from earliest times in the Church, Mary, the mother of Jesus, the archetype of the Church and of all fulfilled Christians, enjoyed a special place of veneration, but also a special power of intercession on behalf of the faithful pilgrims still on this earth?

Mary intimately shared in the life, suffering and death of her Son. The faithful have always instinctively believed that she is now one with him in heaven, sharing in the transformation of body, soul and spirit through the Church's belief in her assumption into glory. Part of Mary's sharing in Christ's glory is a sharing in Jesus' powerful intercession before the Father. As she surrendered at each moment during her earthly life to live according to God's Word, Jesus Christ, so now Mary, above all the saints, continues in her heavenly life to surrender herself to implement God's Word through loving service.

Such Christian belief among the faithful of all ages reassures us, and is a source of great joy, that Mary and the saints and angels now live with full consciousness and understanding of our needs. The Church encourages us to pray to them, teaching us that they are aware of such communication and can intercede for us through the priesthood of Christ, the only high priest. If Paul burned with zeal to win all to Christ (1 Co 9:22), can we ever doubt a similar zeal and loving concern toward us in our needs on the part of Mary and the other saints?

Applications

If we were to take this doctrine of the communion of saints seriously we would find it perfectly natural to walk and talk with these beautiful sisters and brothers of ours, who have gone before us and yet are ever present to us in our daily needs. Milton expressed this belief in a world of holy spirits ever present to us when he wrote: "Millions of spiritual creatures walk the earth unseen, both when we wake and when we sleep" (*Paradise Lost* IV).

In the workings of God we will find, as we perhaps have already found, that we are drawn in fondness and "at homeness" toward certain saints. These become incarnational points in love of opening ourselves to this invisible world of holy spirits. They also come to know and love us with a certain fondness in Christ, that radiates joy from and to each other. The Curate of Ars, St. Jean Vianney, walked in the presence of St. Philomena. Who are your favorite saints? Why are you attracted to them? How have you felt their particular presence and help? Have they been a special joy to you in your "low" moments and in your needs? Does not your devotion to them make the entire body of the triumphant, glorified Christ most real to you?

Devotion to our departed loved ones

If love is the medium or the environment in which we can communicate with those who have departed, then ought we not be able easily to be in touch with our departed loved ones? If they have been a source of great joy while we lived with them on this earth, should our contact with them not bring us also much joy, even daily? Though they may not be saints like those canonized in Christian piety and noted for their heroic virtues and nearness to the Lord, yet there has been a very special loving presence of God in our love relationships with them while they were on this earth. Not only do they look to us for help in their purification and the help needed to burn out the last traces of self-centeredness, but they also have need to show us love, for to the degree that in the new life they enjoy in Christ they have grown to become loving persons, to that degree they stretch out to actuate this love.

The love of God in them still binds them as closely to us as before in the unfolding of our friendship with them on earth. This binding love of Christ makes it possible for us to communicate with them and for them to be in communication with us. This has nothing whatever to do with the occult practice of spiritualism in which one seeks to make contact with a dead member of his or her family through a psychic medium. Such practices are to be avoided as bordering on the magical and do not open one up to the true love of Christ, but to the suggestions of a world of darkness. Our desire is to live in the loving presence of our departed loved ones, because our faith assures us that they still consciously love us and wish to help us. This brings great joy to us every time we are in loving contact with them in their new life.

The help they wish to bring in their relationship with us is the help of Christ himself in answer to our needs unto our happiness. Surely if they honestly wished, while they were on earth with us, to show their love by sharing their knowledge, wisdom and understanding by offering advice, would it be far fetched to believe that they can still share with us their enlightened counsel now? Do we really believe they love us and wish to show us that love now in a far superior way than they showed it while with us on earth?

Then we should not speak of having "lost" a husband, wife, friend, son or daughter, but rather we should find ways of communing with such beloved ones often during the day, as little joyful reminders of them lead us into their spiritual presence. I remember a woman describing to me how she had felt the presence and protective, active love of her deceased husband once when she was driving on an icy road in the dark of night. The car careened out of control and was heading toward the median of the road into the glaring lights of oncoming traffic from the opposite direction. She cried out the name of her husband and immediately sensed his hand on her shoulder. Suddenly a force seemed to take over the wheel in a gentle way, and she felt the car straighten out and begin to move in the proper direction. You undoubtedly have heard of many similar cases of how the name and the presence of a deceased loved one called forth aid in some physical or psychological need.

Heaven already

The whole world around us is permeated with the saints, angels and all our departed loved ones. Then there are so many other beautiful persons whom we never had the opportunity to meet personally on earth, except perhaps through their writings, music, painting, poetry or other accomplishments. The joy of heaven will be that inter-mutuality in loving, giving and sharing with those who freely have surrendered to Christ and wish to share their unique manifestation of God's beauty, as they share themselves with us and we share ourselves with them. This joy of heaven should begin now, as we live the beautiful teaching of the Church on the communion of saints. Then death will never separate us from our beautiful sisters and brothers, our relatives and friends, but it will be the occasion to move into the real world and begin to experience the fulfillment of the prayer of Jesus that he is continually offering to his heavenly Father on behalf of all God's children, that we may all be one in them as Jesus and the Father are one (Jn 17:21-24).

Joy in Dying

One human experience that certainly awaits all of us living on planet earth and that usually takes away whatever joy we have in this life is the prospect of our own future death. Never before in human history has death been so close to all of us, especially through instant satellite communications. We constantly are exposed to this grim reality of human death. Daily we see on TV news coverage, in movies, in our newspapers persons dying. Sometimes we even witness places on our planet where genocides are taking place, wars are wiping out thousands of human beings. Droughts, tornadoes, hurricanes, floods, earthquakes and volcano eruptions bring human deaths to our living rooms. So many people dying, portrayed in a dehumanized, impersonalized manner, tend to numb our sensitivities, and gradually we find ourselves blocking out the certainty that we too will surely die.

The reality is that death is a terrifying upheaval in our human way of existing, in fact, in the only way of living that we have ever experienced. It is a fearful sundering of the only existence we have known up to that moment. It is the most "unnatural" act that we have to undergo in this life. Thus psychologically we learn ways not to think of death or ways of denying that death will ever happen to us. In such ways we can suppress our fears and anxieties. The result is: we have very little joy in an anxious life.

Ways of death-denial

Western culture helps us in this death-denying process. Through our affluence and technology we have fashioned a cult of the comfortable. Who dares think of death or speak of that awful possibility when there is so much to live for! It is all so terribly negative! Arnold Toynbee, the British historian, writes:

Death is "unAmerica"; for, if the fact of death were once admitted to be a reality even in the United States, then it would also have to be admitted that the United States is not the earthly paradise that it is deemed to be (and this is one of the crucial articles of faith in "the American way of life"). Present-day Americans, and other present-day Westerners too in their degree, tend to say, instead of "die," "pass on" or "pass away." (*Man's Concern with Death*, p. 131)

We ignore reminders that we too will surely one day die by throwing ourselves frantically into functional activities, earning lots of money so we can buy symbols of human power. We travel to forget our mortality. We search through various ways for new peak experiences so as never to be bored in our fear of monotony. Movies, sports, our own creative work, hobbies, alcohol, drugs, gambling, over-eating and sex may give us some temporary relief from the universal, gnawing question: after death, then what?

Is there not a connection with our Western obsession with sex and our fear of our own personal death? Dr. Rollo May gives this explanation:

Death is a symbol of ultimate impotence and finiteness, and anxiety arising from this inescapable experience calls forth the struggle to make ourselves infinite by way of sex. . . . Repression of death equals obsession with sex. Sex is the easiest way to prove our vitality, to demonstrate we are still "young," attractive and virile, to prove we are not dead yet. (Cited in Hunt, *Don't Be Afraid to Die*, pp. 17-18)

Wake up from your sleep

I often wonder what would Jesus Christ preach to us modern women and men if he were to return in human form on this earth. I believe he would tell us never to have any fear in life-situations, because his perfect love, the image of the Father's love through their mutual Holy Spirit, would drive out all fear (1 Jn 4:18). From the gospels we find firstly that Jesus preached and would do so today that the kingdom of God, the kingdom of living in the experience of the trinitarian community's love for us, is always breaking in upon us personally and individually. The three divine persons, Father, Son and Holy Spirit, are always present to us, filling us with their self-giving, uncreated energies of love. Entrance into that kingdom brings about a great joy in our relationship with God, with ourselves, with our neighbors and with the entire universe. From this joy flow deep peace and a sense of harmonious unity in our personal oneness with and uniqueness from other human beings and all other creatures, that is yet different from the individuality and uniqueness of the triune persons.

I believe, secondly, that Jesus would seek with great urgency that we would wake up from our hypnotic sleep and arise from the world of illusions of the dead to receive the light of new life in and through our belief in Jesus Christ, God-man. Although we readily acknowledge that we are physically awake in our daily consciousness, yet we live in a certain psychic and spiritual, numbing sleep. Most of us dwell in a world far different from God's free and real world.

The great deception is that we do not realize that we are asleep to God's reality, because our false *ego* has constructed around us a world of illusion. As Christians we are given the possibility to believe in a mystery that our physical death is not the end of our lives, but that we enter into a continuing of the life as we have lived it on this earth. The mode of existence is something we can never really experience until we pass through our physical death. This is possible only through the gift of Jesus to wake us up from our sleep and open us to his eternal life which we now are able to live, as we accept him as our Savior. He wishes to wake us up as he did his friend Lazarus. "Our friend Lazarus is resting. I am going to wake him up" (Jn 11:11).

Jesus would instruct us, thirdly, in our necessity for a conversion, a *metanoia*, as a complete upheaval of all our habitual values rooted in our self-centeredness as the center of our dreamy existence. The seed must die before it can bring forth new and more abundant life (Jn 12:24). If we wish to "passover" to live no longer in illusions but in God's real world of loving harmony which alone can bring us true joy, we must be ready to deny ourselves the satisfaction of our illusory desires (Eph 4:22) and to die to our "old self" in order to find our true life in his life (Mk 8:35).

Fourthly, Jesus would invite us to share in his abundant life that he brings us. He would say to us what he spoke to busy Martha:

> I am the resurrection and the life; whoever believes in me, even if he dies, will live, and everyone who lives and believes in me will never die. Do you believe this? (Jn 11:25-26)

Thomas Merton writes about the joy that comes when we live our true life in union with God, who is life:

> The only true joy on earth is to escape from the prison of our own false self, and enter by love into union with the Life who dwells and sings within the essence of every creature and in the core of our own souls. In his love we possess all things and enjoy fruition of them, finding him in them all. (*New Seeds of Contemplation*, p. 25)

Choosing life now

What great sadness, lack of joy and meaninglessness in our lives do we experience when we freely wish to remain in our somnolent state of darkness and refuse to accept the light of Christ! We continue for so many years of our earthly lives living in an unreal world that we, not God, have created. We set up a world of disharmony, chaos and utter disorder. We worship ourselves as God, the beginning and end of the world we have created. We live independently of God. But this is to live the gigantic *lie* and not in God's truth, where he is the center of all his created world.

The more we drive out true joy by living according to our false self, the deeper we move away from God's real world. We freely lock ourselves in an inescapable prison of selfishness, and the more meaningless will be our lives. Sartre claimed that other people were hell. But hell is our own creation, and we are our own judges and prosecutors. We turn through sin from life and live in death. We unceasingly insist that God and the world of his saints are false, and only our unhappy world is true, causing ourselves yet more pain, since we are in disharmony with the source of our very being and the goal of all our true strivings.

Living in God's love

We begin to drive out of our lives unhappiness and meaningless-ness when we listen to the indwelling Word of God leading us into his life by challenging us to let go of our selfish *ego* and our unreal world and to take the risk to live in love of God and neighbor. It is then that we begin to enter here and now in this life into a share of God's kingdom of heaven. Realizing that heaven is living already by God's grace and our cooperation according to God's "truth and love" (Ep 4:15), we accept the exciting journey of an eternal life of growing into seeing Christ in all things and all things in him (Col 3:11).

What a difference in our daily choices to act on the faith that our eternal happiness in the life to come is being determined now by our dynamic living out of our death to selfishness and our rising to a new oneness in the risen Christ. The truths revealed to us by Christ through his Church about life after death are gifts of grace calling us to assert our precious God-given free will to live in each thought, word and deed in love.

For love freely given by us has the gentle power to span all distances, all times and to conquer the seeming abyss that separates us on earth from those who have passed beyond the grace into eternal life. In the beautiful words of Blessed Robert Southwell, the sixteenth century English Jesuit martyr and poet, we experience that "Not where I breathe do I live but where I love." The love of God abounds in our hearts through the Spirit that is given to us (Rm 5:5). Joy now and in the life to come becomes God's gift that accompanies love of God and neighbor.

A Christian view of death

Karl Rahner, in his classical work *On the Theology of Death*, employs a more holistic, biblical concept of the whole being dying, and not merely the physical body. He insists that it is rather a whole person that undergoes death. Thus he avoids the image of the soul "leaving" this world and going up into a spiritual world, losing all relationships with the material world once the body is dead. He writes:

> It should rather be borne in mind that, even in her lifetime, as informing the body, the spiritual soul is an open system toward the world. It might also be remembered with profit that natural philosophy finds it almost impossible to restrict the idea of the human "body" to what is covered by the skin. The spiritual soul, moreover, through her essential relationship to the body, is basically open to the world in such a manner that she is never a monad without windows, but always in communication with the whole of the world. (p. 30)

Why do we have to die?

From scripture and the continued teaching of the Church, death is seen as a result of sin. In original justice, that is, the way God had intended us human beings to live in relationships to God and the rest of created nature, grace was to bring us into a deep communion with God. The sin of Adam and Eve was their living in independence outside of a loving obedience to God's wishes. This broke radically the union between God and his human children.

Before sin entered into the human race, human beings may have been able to live immune from death, or, if they were to die, such a transition into a higher level of conscious evolution would have been likened more to a sleep than the violent upheaval it is now because of sin.

Rahner gives us the basis for a Christian joy in confronting our own personal, physical death. Death is something passively suffered. It happens to all of us; even Jesus and Mary, his mother, underwent this. This is the biological aspect that brings a definitive end to our "natural" way of existing through a material, quantified body in space and time relationships to the rest of the material world around us.

Through such natural relationships as a bodied-person, we become persons, as we freely choose to make of ourselves that unique person, capable of giving ourselves freely in love to God and neighbor. It is this personal element that varies for each of us, as we face our own death. What you experience on the biological level is passively something you share with all other human beings. We can do very little as we "suffer" death as it happens to us.

Actively accepting death unto higher life

But death as an "act" is a human being confronting death and freely ordering this act toward God as one's ultimate end. Rahner's words are important if we wish to reconcile suffering, and yet at the same time we can enter the dying process with Christian joy, the gift of the Holy Spirit:

> But how he dies his death, and how he understands it, depends on the decision of his freedom. Here he does not carry something imposed on him, but what he chooses himself. That is to say: in the deed of the dying existence, man is necessarily free in his attitude toward death. Although he has to die, he is asked how he wishes to do it. For, existence conscious of itself

must unavoidably see the end. It sees this and all through life, perhaps dimly and not explicitly. It may happen that it will purposely avoid looking at it, or it will simply overlook it (but still will realize it all the same). Inasmuch as man freely takes upon himself this existence tending toward the end, he also freely accepts the movement toward the end. (*On the Theology of Death*, pp. 94-95)

We are like the first man, Adam, and the first woman, Eve, insofar as we too have free will to take our life in hand and freely affirm ourselves in total self-surrendering love to God in joy and freedom. We can shape our being from the depths of our personhood that can still be part of death as we know it after sin. It should be this free act, not only on your deathbed but throughout all your earthly life, that imparts to your Christian life and death in Christ's eternal, risen life a free choice that conquers sin and death (Rm 8:2).

It is this attitude that brings to us deep joy in the time of actual death, in spite of the passive elements that may bring much suffering to us. Jesus conquered sin and death, and you can now scorn death since it no longer has any sting or victory over you (1 Co 15:55).

We die as we live

The earthly life of Jesus, from what we can learn from the gospel narratives, was a preparation, in each conscious moment of his life, for his final death. Each choice was made in ever-growing freedom to place his life, every thought, word and deed, under the good pleasure of his Father. He always did what most pleased his heavenly Father (Jn 8:29).

Freedom for Jesus as for you is God's gift through the Spirit of love, but it is won by a great struggle, wherein the isolated self surrenders to the true self in living in love for God and neighbor. Jesus gives us the model and the graceful strength to live and die as he did. "The Father loves me, because I lay down my life in order to take it up again. No one takes it from me; I lay it down of my own free will'' (Jn 10:17). Jesus reaches his full human potential as he freely surrenders his life to the Father. He suffers on the cross as any other crucified person would. Yet he actively brings together his whole lifetime of freely surrendering in love as a gift to his Father in every thought, word and action.

The glory of the cross

The secret of an authentic Christian, joyful death, even amid much suffering, lies in the power of the cross. It is a logic and wisdom that go beyond the rational control of our human nature. ''The language of the cross may be illogical to those who are not on the way to salvation, but those of us who are on the way see it as God's power to save'' (1 Co 1:18). Paul tells us of the power and the wisdom of God that make what is impossible to us possible by God's grace: ''God's own foolishness is wiser than human wisdom and God's weakness is stronger than human strength'' (1 Co 1:25).

The wisdom of the cross stands as the parting of the Christian's view toward death and that of someone not informed by God's wisdom, made manifest in Christ Jesus. This is the paradox Jesus lived and taught us to live: lose your life (in love) and you will find it. Hold on to it, and you will lose it. Joy is possible in dying because, as we die in Christ, we already have eternal life. And no one can take this from us ever!

> Whoever wishes to come after me must deny himself, take up his cross, and follow me. For whoever wishes to save his life will lose it, but whoever loses his life for my sake will find it. (Mt 16:24-25)

Jesus Risen: Our True Joy

Today we are plagued with the problem of the meaning of our human existence, before mounting invisible powers of evil in our society, along with our burden of guilt for the disharmony within ourselves and around us in the world. Death threatens any meaningful existence and destroys our joy. With so much to live for, we want to live longer than previous human beings have done. But through technology we see more of death all about us. Hence our preoccupation with the problem of death and dying, which brings even greater sadness to our lives.

Jesus lived and taught that in order to attain the full, true human life and to share joyfully in God's eternal life, self-centeredness had to be abandoned. He lived for others and freely died for all of us. He shows us an image of God emptying himself out in the nature of a servant (Ph 2:6 ff). Paul shows us the reason for Christ's death: "He indeed died for all, so that those who live might no longer live for themselves but for him who for their sake died and was raised" (2 Co 5:15).

As death out of love for us brought Jesus' resurrection, so the pattern for the Christian life is the same: We must die to sin in order to live in a newness of life. "For if we have grown into union with him through a death like his, we shall also be united with him in the resurrection. We know that our old self was crucified with him, so that our sinful body might be done away with, that we might no longer be in slavery to sin" (Rm 6:5-6).

Ultimate meaningfulness

Jesus has taken the sting out of death and given us meaningfulness beyond this life that stretches into eternal life. He is the ultimate source of our lasting joy, in this life and in the life to come, because he has broken "the power of death" (2 Tm 1:10). The good news is that God so loved this world as to give us his only Son, that we might believe in him as the saving Lord and thus share in God's eternal life (Jn 3:16).

God's love is the ultimate meaningfulness beyond all human, rational explanations of what is really real. But this is a love that is self-emptying, *kenotic* in its outpouring of oneself in self-sacrifice for the other. No rational assault upon life's ultimate meaning can ever effect a surrender to God's love, that covers itself only with darkness when our mere probing intellect attacks the mystery of life.

And yet to the broken ones of this world, who humbly cry out to God for the coming of his love incarnated, Jesus Christ, into their lives, this mystery of love that *death is resurrection* is revealed. It becomes a living experience that cannot be taught and yet that grows into the fullness of reality, as one enters into the exodus-passover experience of moving away from self-centeredness to God-centeredness.

God's miracle

The resurrection of Christ is the central mystery of our Christian faith and the source of all our continued joy. The resurrection is God's constant miracle, meeting us in the sordid brokenness but also in the limited joys and moments of self-fulfillment, in the many deaths and risings from the dead that make up the story of this day, and of tomorrow, and of every day of our earthly existence. Jesus in his body, of which we are his members, can be raised in this moment to newness of life. The resurrection of Jesus, the head, of his Church, the members, you and me as individuals, finding our uniqueness precisely by discovering ourselves in the corporateness of that body, is now taking place, as we unveil and yield to the power of the risen Lord in the context of our place and time in history.

The touch of the risen Lord can change the suffering of body or mind or spirit that you are undergoing into a new sharing of his eternal life. The recent loss of your loved one can be a new release from selfish possession to loving and prayerful presence to him or her in a new union that passes from death to resurrection. Your financial worries and anxieties can be a death-to-new-life, as you seek the kingdom of God before all else and experience Christ's new resurrectional life.

Laughter and joy amidst apparent absurdity can be signs of not taking ourselves too seriously as candidates for the Godhead, but of experiencing God's raising power in our weakness.

The paradox of the cross

God has brought Jesus back from the dead "to become the great shepherd of the sheep by the blood that sealed an eternal covenant" (Heb 13:30). Everywhere on the pages of the New Testament we find joy expressed, because Jesus has suffered and died for love of his followers and has gone forward into a completely new existence, which he now makes it possible for his disciples to share. "Do not be afraid, I am the first and the last, the one who lives. Once I was dead, but now I am alive forever and ever. I hold the keys to death and the netherworld" (Rv 1:17-18).

Paul shows the intimate connection between Jesus' death and resurrection and our own justification when he writes of "Jesus who was put to death for our sins and raised to life to justify us" (Rm 4:25). Jesus "died and was raised to life" (2 Co 5:15), in order that we might have eternal life. The resurrection of Christ is not only pivotal to the life and mission of Jesus; it is fundamental to God's actions throughout all human history. That is why Paul saw so clearly the centrality of Jesus' resurrection: "If Christ has not been raised, you are still in your sins" (1 Co 15:17).

Paradoxes of Christianity

We can highlight in general why Christ's resurrection is the key to a new creation, which we are now privileged to live in continued joy, by listing from the New Testament the symbols that paradoxically bring death and resurrection, a life in suffering but also one of joy. Jesus preached about death-life, darkness-light, bondage-freedom. He came among human beings and lived such paradoxes. He was the light that came into our darkness, even though the darkness did not comprehend him (Jn 1:9-11). He came to bring life, and that more abundantly, to those who were sick and dying (Jn 10:10). He was the power in whom all things were created and made (Jn 1:2; Col 1:16), yet he appeared in weakness, crucified and emptied out on the cross for love of us. In his humiliations he was lifted up (Jn 12:32) and exalted in glory by his Father (Ph 2:10). He descended into our world, tempted in all things, save sin (Heb 4:15), in order that we might ascend with him into heavenly glory (Heb 4:8-10).

His defeat on the cross by the powers of evil led to eternal victory over sin and death. His shame turned to glory, and he holds out to us the same possibility of suffering with him, in order that we might also enter into glory with him (Rm 8:17).

He was the second Adam who offset the fall of the first Adam, and he now makes it possible for us to put off the old self and put on the new man (Eph 4:22; 2 Co 5:18). Through his resurrectional life, living in us through the release of his Spirit, we can become "spiritual" persons (Rm 8: 9-11) by putting off the perishable and the corruptible and by living as already in the incorruptible life of the Spirit. He has destroyed sin and death and has restored us to become children of the heavenly Father (Rm 8:16; Ga 4:6).

We have been baptized into his death, and he has raised us to new life. He has gone away from this earth, and yet he remains always with us, as he and the Father come and abide within us to share their trinitarian life with us through their mutual Spirit of love (Jn 14:23). To live in the mystery of Jesus' resurrection is to allow his victory to exercise daily a transforming power in our lives. This victory is the experienced knowledge of the Father and Jesus, his Son, through the Holy Spirit, in their infinite love always being poured out into our hearts (Rm 5:5).

It is this knowledge that brings joy and eternal life and a share even now in the victory of his resurrection (Jn 17:30). This knowledge, received in prayer, is experienced freshly every time you and I live in self-sacrificing love for another person. Only in such a manner can we experientially know the infinite love of God in Jesus, that drove him in dying for us to empty himself unto the last drop of blood, as he imaged on the cross the perfect love of the heavenly Father for us.

A new time and a new space

What brought ineffable joy to the members of the first Christian community in Jerusalem that had experienced Jesus as truly risen from the dead was that he could be present to them more intimately by his resurrection than he had ever been before his death. He continues to be present in his new "time" that Paul calls *kairos* and in a new space that scriptures call "heart," not by being resuscitated, but by his having been truly risen from the dead. For the early Christians and for us who build our faith upon theirs everything now is new! There is a new immediacy to us, as Jesus passes over the limits of earthly time and space and enters into a new age, a new creation.

The whole work of the risen Jesus is to release the fullness of the Holy Spirit as God's personalized gift of love. Love has the power to catch up space and time and transform them into an experience of two persons becoming one in spacelessness that knows no harshness of ticking time. In love you burst the limitations of confining time and space. You soar through the firmaments of past, present and future, as you learn to rest in the ever-abiding *now* moment of loving union with the indwelling Father, risen Son and Holy Spirit. No time can lock you into a limitation of past, present or future when you live in the power of the risen Lord. No place can hold you within its painful grasp, as you stretch to touch the ecstasy of eternity in the already *now!*

John of the Cross explains how love transcends the limits of our earthly bodies. "The soul lives where it loves rather than in the body which it animates, because it has not its life in the body, but rather gives it to the body and lives through love in that which it loves" (*The Spiritual Canticle*, stanza 8).

Jesus received the fullness of the Father's Spirit at the moment when he passed over the limits of earthly time and space and entered into a new age. Jesus meets us now in his eternal now (*kairos*) moment, which touches us in our historical (*chronos*) moment. In this moment of brokenness in our history Jesus comes with the Father through their Spirit of love to lift us to a similar "resurrection" unto new life, as in his Spirit we live out of love and in joy.

The apostles never yearned in nostalgia for the historical past times in which they had experienced Jesus before his death. They were experiencing him in a progression forward to a new way, in which they could live in his victory always, night and day. If they only wished, they need never be separated from the indwelling Father, Son and Holy Spirit. Heaven was already with them! No longer was Jesus physically present to them as before in one limited place in Palestine. Now, wherever they went, they carried this transforming, conquering power within them.

Heart space

What brings us great joy is that Jesus by his resurrectional presence invites you and me to enter into a new space that scripture calls the "heart." It is there in the Spirit's faith, hope and love that we experience our true self in being "in Christ Jesus." In the space of our hearts, in the deepest reaches of our consciousness, permeated by the Spirit's grace, we encounter the risen Jesus in the spaceless space of his healing love.

Jesus by his resurrection undoes in his own person, and in our lives as well, what Adam, the first parent of the human race, did by sin. Jesus enters into a new birth by his resurrection and shares that new life with us, his members. The signs of our earthly time and space, into which Adam and his progeny were immersed, are death and corruption. The signs of the New Adam and his new creation are an ever-growing youthfulness and increase in life, beauty and happiness.

A new birth to new life

He who was eternally one with God (Ph 2:6) came into a new birth at Easter. He "was proclaimed Son of God in all his power through his resurrection from the dead" (Rm 1:4). Paul preached: "The one whom God has raised up, however, has not experienced corruption" (Ac 13:37).

Time is reversed, as Jesus, through his resurrection, is eternally being begotten. Christmas is caught forever in the Easter event. Jesus Christ can no longer grow older, nor can he be subjected to corruption and death. He is being renewed daily in glory and power. His dominion extends to all nations and to all parts of the world.

Time and space have been redeemed. The past times and places have been healed of their limitations and brokenness. And now time and space have been carried forward into the future, but a future of ever-increasing life and deeper joy.

Transformation

Our present time and space, by the presence of the risen Lord and our cooperation with him and his Spirit, have no longer a negative power over us. But more positively our faith, hope and love for the risen Lord lead us to a new framework, in which we are called to bring the transforming power of Christ's new life into our very own time and space. Having experienced the healing love of the risen

Jesus living within us and abiding there with his eternal Father through his Spirit of love, we are empowered to take our broken moment in the history of the human race and our place in that disjointed history in order to transform them into a new age.

We are called to be Christ's ambassadors and reconcilers of this shattered world (2 Co 5:17-20) to bring all things to God. The old time and space are still with us, and we journey in them along with the broken ones of this world. Yet, the good news that Jesus is risen is bringing through us his power and glory to uplift and transform this tired and dying world into the new creation, that is to become the total Christ.

This Christ is now in pilgrimage through a dark and arid desert. His body in time and space is broken, but it is constantly being healed by the Spirit's love. He who said, "I am the resurrection and the life, whoever believes in me, even if he dies, will live, and everyone who lives and believes in me will never die" (Jn 11:25-26), has not left us to struggle alone. He is with us, and we already live in his power and glory.

Jesus in his resurrectional presence is close to us in the very context of our disjointed time and space. He is ready to release his Spirit who allowed him in his humanity to transcend the limitations of human, historical time and space. This same Spirit convinces us that the heavenly Father, who has loved us with an everlasting love, loves us in his perfectly fulfilled word-made-flesh, Jesus Christ.

We are the people "who were once brought into the light, and tasted the gift from heaven, and received a share of the Holy Spirit, and appreciated the good message of God and the powers of the world to come" (Heb 6:4-5). We are humbled and joyful in believing that those powers of the world to come are already given to us in this vale of tears by Jesus risen. "All power in heaven and on earth has been given to me. Go, therefore, and make disciples of all nations, baptizing them in the name of the Father, and of the Son, and of the Holy Spirit. And behold, I am with you always, until the end of the age" (Mt 28:18-20).

Our joy is full, as we experience that we belong to Christ the victor, the *Pantocrator,* who has conquered sin, death, and all the limitations of time and space that Paul lumps together in the one word, *corruption.* All our actions we seek to perform in his name, in return for his eternal love for us. His power, wisdom, grace and strength, in a word his Spirit, becomes our sharing in Jesus' resurrection.

Time and space still hold us in their grasp, but now we know that we live in Christ and, therefore, even now we live forever in eternal life. Jesus Christ is present within you as an inner light that powerfully dissipates your indwelling darkness. What dark clouds of selfishness cover us from within us and impede us from letting the light of Christ transform us into light! What fears are locked deeply within us! Such fears spawn other forms of fear as doubts, anxieties, dread, worries, hatred, anger, horror, fight or terror of the past, the present, the future.

The birthing of your unique I-ness

Jesus Christ is present as risen, living deep down within you. Your true self, that alone can bring you full meaningfulness, is there waiting to be born into his life. The Spirit of the risen Jesus hovers over this inner chaos and darkness which resist that birthing of yourself into Christ. Your true self cannot be brought to birth by yourself. Your identity as an *I* can only be discovered in the *Thou* of Jesus Christ in whom you find your full reason for being. He alone is the Divine Physician who possesses the fullness of life in himself, because he is the true image of the invisible God.

It is only through the Holy Spirit, released by the indwelling, risen Jesus, that you and I can know the full Jesus Christ and our true selves in our loving oneness with him (1 Jn 3:24). This Spirit of love fills us with faith in God's great love in Christ Jesus, and in that living and loving Christ abiding intimately within us. We are filled with hope by the Spirit that the risen and loving Christ abides intimately within us. We are filled with hope by the Spirit that the risen Lord has conquered sin and death, and we meet this indwelling, risen Lord in all of our darkness and inauthenticity. The Spirit fills us with the hopeful realization that our fully integrated person, the one we should be by God's unique love for each of us, can be realized only by the interacting, loving relationships of the Father, Son and Holy Spirit dwelling within us.

Today: the first day of eternity

To let go and live in the mystery of love is to touch the wounds of the risen Lord and know that God is raising his Son to new power and glory. The miracle of the resurrection is happening at every moment of our daily lives, as we are open to God's Word speaking in his creative act of raising us up to new levels of sharing in his resurrectional, transforming love.

Today is always becoming a new beginning, the first day of eternity, and it is happening as we live death-resurrection in this present, *now* moment. We can interpret the beautiful words, "As long as we love one another, God will live in us and his love will be complete in us" (1 Jn 4:12), to mean: "As long as we love another, Christ is more completely being risen and manifested in power and glory on this earth."

We will stretch out in hope for the fullness of Christ's coming in glory, as we open up to the miracle of Christ's living, resurrectional presence in the concrete details of life's banality, monotony, brokenness, and seeming meaninglessness. He will lead us from death to life, from non-reality to reality, from the darkness of fear to the light of a new experience in his resurrection. The New Jerusalem is being fashioned now, and in joy and peace we can say *no* to Babylon and *yes* to God's new creation. Rooted in the human situation, we live in love and seek for the New City that awaits us and, yet, mysteriously is already here among us, as we live out our death to embrace a new level of even now sharing in the resurrection of Jesus.

To the degree that we have entered into his death-resurrection, we will be able to extend the resurrectional, transforming power of Jesus into the material world around us. Jesus risen becomes more risen in his body, the Church, as we and others allow him to effect the reconciliation of the divided world through our creative efforts. He hands on to us this great work of reconciliation of a world that is torn by dissension and separation. Whatever work you do in love to make this world a bit better, on any level of political, social, scientific, technological, artistic endeavor, you are contributing to the fulfillment of this world. Let us turn to see how the Spirit of Jesus risen releases him in our world in and through our gifts received from his Holy Spirit.

The Holy Spirit's Gift of Joy

One of the great and very popular saints of the Russian Church known for his constant spirit of joy is Seraphim of Sarov (+1833). He lived most of his monastic life as a hermit in a forest in central Russia near Kursk, where he followed the ascetical and mystical life of the early hermits of Egypt and Syria. Only after years of ascetical purification did Seraphim close his life of complete silence and contemplation in order to share his joy as an "elder" or spiritual director of monastic nuns and lay persons.

He radiated joy as a luminous light that made his purified soul translucent to an outsider who beheld him. He met each person with a humble, joyous salutation of "My joy!" His constant teaching was this which he addressed to his spiritual disciple, the layman Nicholas Motovilov: "The true aim of our Christian life is to acquire the Holy Spirit of God. . . . The Holy Spirit itself enters our souls, and this presence with our spirit of the Triune Majesty is only granted to us through our own assiduous acquisition of the Holy Spirit, which prepares in our soul and body a throne for the all-creative presence of God with our spirit according to his irrevocable word: 'I will dwell in them and walk in them; and I will be their God, and they shall be my people.' "

We cannot become divinized children of God without being regenerated and transformed by the power and glory of the Holy Spirit. The greatest gift of the heavenly Father to us is truly, and always will be, his Son made flesh, Jesus Christ. Yet, the gift the Son gives us is the Holy Spirit, that we may know him and understand all he has said and done as recorded in the gospels and bear witness to him as our Lord and Savior (Jn 14:26; 15:26-27).

Jesus promised his disciples that through the power of his Spirit he would return to them as the risen Lord, and they would be filled with a joy that no one could ever take from their hearts. "So you also are now in anguish. But I will see you again and your hearts will rejoice and no one will take your joy away from you . . . so that your joy may be complete" (Jn 16:22-24).

The Spirit reveals the love of the Father

We can understand the nature and work of the Holy Spirit if we first recall the work of the Spirit in the human life of Jesus, which is similar to his work in us. In the humanity of Jesus the Father poured his Spirit of love into his being. The baptism of Jesus in the Jordan gives us a model of the progress of Jesus' human development over his whole life, climaxing in the cross and resurrection.

Jesus receives a vision as he comes out of the water, seeing the Spirit as a gentle dove and hearing his Father declare from on high: "You are my beloved Son; with you I am well pleased" (Mk 1:11). The heavens opened, and Jesus was made aware in his human consciousness that he is hearing his heavenly Father and seeing the Holy Spirit come upon him as the Father's gift.

Deep down the human Jesus is swept up into an ecstatic oneness with the Father. Like the water that fell over his human body, so the love of the Father for him as his beloved Son cascaded over him and covered him with his glory. Heaven and earth had been closed by the first sin of man and woman in Eden. Now God's communicating presence has passed through the barrier of sin, and Jesus, God's holiness, stands within our human family.

The Spirit brings Jesus, not in this one moment of his baptism, but in every moment of his conscious, human existence to a greater joyful and peaceful assurance that the Father truly loved him. The Spirit gives to the human Jesus the determination to be perfect as the heavenly Father is perfect (Mt 5:48), and he gives him the loving power to fulfill in all events that desire.

The power and glory of the Spirit

Wherever the Spirit operates in the Old and New Testaments he operates as the agent or face of God's loving power. The Spirit is the creative force of God moving toward chaos, darkness and death and drawing the "void" into a sharing of God's being (Gn 1:2). The Spirit is a powerful wind stirring stillness into a dynamic new life. He is the one who gives new hearts (Ezk 36:26), anointing kings, judges and prophets with wisdom and knowledge. Jesus received the Spirit as a power, enabling him to preach, teach, heal and perform miracles.

But in his death-resurrection Jesus is raised up by the Spirit into the fullness of power. When Paul writes that Jesus was raised by the power and glory of God, he means that it is the Holy Spirit, who is the power and the glory of God, who raised Jesus. "Yes, but he was crucified through weakness, and still he lives now through the power of God" (1 Co 13:4).

The power is the Spirit, but he imparts the fullness to the risen Lord, who can now give us a share in that power and glory. "All power in heaven and on earth has been given to me. Go, therefore, and make disciples of all nations" (Mt 28:18-19).

Because Jesus has the fullness of God's glory, he can send us the fullness of the Spirit, who allows us to grow into greater and greater glory. If we are united to the glorified Jesus Christ, we are to that degree being transformed into an image of his glory through the same Spirit.

> All of us, gazing with unveiled face on the glory of the Lord,
> are being transformed into the same image from glory to glory,
> as from the Lord who is the Spirit. (2 Co 3:18)

The Last Age

The key to our Christian joy, the gift of the Holy Spirit, of the risen Jesus (Ga 5:22), lies in the fact that the Last Age has burst upon us in Jesus' resurrection. Jesus risen is the fullness of all things, "the first born of all creation" (Col 1:17). He makes it possible for all of us, if we live in him, to share even now in his new life and resurrection (1 Jn 11:25). He is the prototype of our future inheritance, the first fruits of those who sleep (1 Co 15:20). If we accept him as the Son of God the Father, the *Kyrios* or Lord of the universe, our eternal high priest, who mightily offers himself without ceasing to the Father on our behalf and to us as our food and drink, we shall have eternal life, and he himself will raise us up also on the last day (Jn 6:40).

One resurrection

If the Holy Spirit was the agent through whom the Father raised Jesus to be life-giving to the world, Jesus can pour out this same Spirit in fullness upon us and even now give us a share in his inheritance (Eph 1:14). We are thus in the fullness of joy, privileged to participate through the same Spirit in the risen life of Christ. We are redeemed, made justified and are risen as we share in his death-resurrection of total submission in love to the Father through his Son in his Spirit of love.

We really are children of God

The Spirit that the risen Jesus sends by asking his Father in glory is seen as the loving force of God himself, divinizing all who are open to receive his gift. This holiness given to us to transform us into heirs of God, true children of God (Rm 8:15), is the very indwelling of God's Spirit taking possession of us Christians, as he penetrates our mind, our thoughts, all our actions with the very divine life of God.

John, the beloved disciple of Jesus, cannot get over the miracle of our regeneration, not by water alone but by the Spirit (Jn 3:3-5). "See what love the Father has bestowed on us that we may be called the children of God. Yet so we are" (1 Jn 3:1). Paul never ceases to describe the main work of the Spirit as bringing us into a new life, a life in Jesus which regenerates us into true children of God: "You are in the Spirit, if only the Spirit of God dwells in you. . . . If the Spirit of the one who raised Jesus from the dead dwells in you, the one who raised Christ from the dead will give life to your mortal bodies also, through his Spirit that dwells in you" (Rm 8:9, 11).

Such a loving presence, so immediately experienced as an indwelling love, fills us with unending joy and an inner dignity touching all human relationships of body, soul and spirit. "Do you know that your body is a temple of the Holy Spirit within you, whom you have from God, and that you are not your own? For you have been purchased at a price. Therefore glorify God in your body" (1 Co 6:19-20).

How can you and I ever again be lonely in the experience of the indwelling Spirit, who witnesses within us by his gifts of faith, hope and love that the Trinity dwells literally within us and loves us with an infinite love? We possess the fullness of the triune God, living and acting in love within us at all times, twenty-four hours of our waking and sleeping, day and night. God cannot come to us in any fuller way than he, the community of love of Father, Son and Holy Spirit, is already living within us. The Spirit brings this new life to its fullness in the proportion that we allow the Spirit to become normative in guiding us Christians to make choices according to the mind of Christ.

A new freedom

Paul was aware of the freeing power of the Holy Spirit as an ongoing process of leading us out of slavery from sin and death and the law into true liberty as children of God. "Now this Lord is the Spirit, and where the Spirit of the Lord is, there is freedom" (2 Co 3:18). Paul applies the word Spirit to the divine power, the Holy

Spirit, sent by God through the merits of Christ and his intercession to effect our sanctification or *christification* of ourselves into Christ.

Paul assigns to the Holy Spirit the character, initiative and salvific action proper to a person. Through his personal experience "in the Spirit," he had discovered the world of the Spirit. It was for him a living "in newness of life" (Rm 6:4). The work of the Spirit is to create this new life in Christ in us Christians. As we become alive by the Spirit, so, Paul exhorts us, then we must walk by the Spirit (Ga 5:16, 26). Christians are *pneumatikoi*, spiritualized by the Spirit, since the primary function of the Spirit is to create this new life in Christ.

Paul sees the world tied together in a hope of being set free from its slavery to decadence, "in hope that creation itself would be set free from slavery to corruption and share in the glorious freedom of the children of God" (Rm 8:20-21). We do not possess the fullness of his gift of joy. But we have come into the "first fruits of the Spirit" (Rm 8:23). Still we have the pledge and guarantee of its completion (2 Co 1:22; Eph 1:14). Thus we can see that for Paul the phrases "in the Spirit" and "in Christ" complement one another.

Guided by the Spirit

We can enjoy the Spirit's gift of joy when we surrender ourselves to being guided by the indwelling Spirit. You and I are caught between two forces: the power of evil and the Spirit of Christ; between the unspiritual in us and the spiritual. We are to live according to the Spirit, the new principle of Christ-like operations within us. The Spirit has created this new life of Christ living within us. We are now to be "spiritual," guided by the Spirit, by turning always within to be moved by God's love. No longer is there an extrinsic code of morality, a Judaic law or any other law operating exclusively. Paul gives us the discernment to see whether we are being guided by the Holy Spirit:

In contrast, the fruit of the Spirit is love, joy, peace, patience, kindness, generosity, faithfulness, gentleness, self-control. Against such there is no law. Now those who belong to Christ Jesus have crucified their flesh with its passions and desires. If we live in the Spirit, let us also follow the Spirit. (Ga 5:22-25)

Only the Spirit of the risen Christ can bring us into true freedom with its accompanying true joy. This highest, human freedom is self-determination in the inmost depths of our being where the Trinity dwells as our center. This freedom is opposed to every kind of external determination which is a force or compulsion from without or from within. We enter into true self-determination only when, in the depths of our meaning, we touch God's Spirit, who releases our spirit to become a loving movement in freedom toward others. True self-determination and self-giving love to others become synonymous and are the freeing work of the Holy Spirit.

In prayer, the Spirit comes to our spirit and bears united witness that we are truly loved, as the Father loves his eternal Son (Rm 8:15). God's very own dynamic current of love, between Father and Son, catches us up and regenerates us into new created beings, ever-more consciously aware of our inner dignity of being so privileged as to be loved infinitely by God. We carry the actual love of God, the Holy Spirit, in our hearts. This love is operating at all times, even when we sleep. The Spirit dominates our spirit, as we seek that inner revolution of our mind to yield to God's Word through the Spirit's love.

Turned in loving service toward others

As we experience deep down the Spirit as the love of God for us in Christ Jesus, that same Spirit brings forth his fruit and gifts, so that we are turned outward toward others in love, "for the love of Christ impels us" (2 Co 5:14). Not only does the Spirit bring about a transformation in our consciousness that we are loved constantly by an infinitely loving Trinity, but that same Holy Spirit is the loving energy that allows us to love others with his very own love.

Now we can accomplish what sin in our members (Rm 7:23) prevented us from doing under our own power. We can now fulfill the two commandments of God: to love God with our whole heart and to love our neighbor as ourselves. We begin to live on a new level of being. We perceive ourselves in a new, joyous light. We walk in that inner dignity, all because of what Jesus Christ has done. "For we are his handiwork, created in Christ Jesus for the good works that God has prepared in advance, that we should live in them" (Eph 2:10).

We see the same world that we looked upon daily before, but now we see "inside." We see that all others are loved infinitely and uniquely by the persons of the Trinity, even though those human persons may not have experienced that same Spirit of love within themselves. We understand by the gift of the Spirit's understanding that we really are one with them. We "intuit" the Word of God, the Logos, in each person to discover that unique personhood in God's eternal creation of her or him in Christ, his Word, as the Spirit has revealed our uniqueness in the same Logos of God.

How can we now hurt anyone, since all persons are our brothers and sisters, and we all belong to Christ's body? How can we judge others who in their ignorance do not realize who they really are? How can we live by violence of any sort, even toward God's creatures of animals, birds, fish, plants and trees and all of the sub-human cosmos, if we are listening gently to Christ's Spirit speak to us of how to live by God's loving energies in each circumstance?

The Spirit unifies prayer and action

By contemplation given us by the Spirit, we can already "see" in ourselves the power of the risen Lord, working to transform us into a oneness with Christ and with the world around us. We can also see the power of the Lord Jesus working in the lives of all human persons, regardless of what culture, religion, race or color. The Spirit fills us with Christ's hope and a joyful optimism, as he points out to us the risen Christ working in a constant process of evolving through the basic goodness in all beings made according to the image of God.

As we toil painstakingly over the little plot of this universe entrusted to us, we are buoyed up by the vision that God's material world has not been conceived by God to be destroyed, but to be transfigured and brought into its fullness in and by the Spirit of the risen Jesus. Freed by the Spirit from self-hate and insecurity, from all fears and anxieties, so that we can become the risen presence of Jesus in the world, we go forth at each moment contemplating and acting in the presence and for the glory of the Trinity. Whatever we do is done for God's glory, is prayer and action transforming by the Spirit the void and chaos into fullness and harmony of love.

Conclusion

I would wish to conclude these chapters on Christian joy by quoting *Hymn 44 of Divine Love* written by Symeon the New Theologian (+1022).

> Being God, the divine Spirit refashions completely
> those whom he receives within himself.
> He makes them completely anew.
> He renews them in an amazing manner.
> How can he avoid taking on something
> of the same filth of them?
> Not any more than fire takes on the black of iron;
> but on the contrary it gives to it all of its own properties.
> So likewise the divine Spirit, incorruptible,
> gives incorruptibility.
> Being immortal, he gives immortality.
> Because he is light that never sets,
> he transforms all of them into light

in whom he comes down and dwells.
And because he is life, he bestows life to all
as he is of the same nature as Christ,
being of the same essence as well as the same in glory,
and being united with him,
he forms them absolutely similar in Christ.
For the Master is not jealous
that mortals should appear equal to himself by divine grace,
that he does not disclaim as unworthy
his servants from becoming like to him.
But rather he is happy, and he rejoices
in seeing all of us,
from mere human to become by grace
as he was and is by nature.
For he is our Benefactor,
and he wishes that all of us become what he himself is.
For if we are not strictly like unto him,
how can we be united to him as he said?
How indeed can we remain in him
if we are not such as he is?
How will he abide in us if we are not similar to him?
Therefore, as you wisely understand this,
hasten to receive the Spirit,
who comes from God and is divine,
in order that you may become such
as my words have explained,
heavenly and divine, such as the Master spoke of
in order to become heirs of the heavenly kingdom forever. . . .
Run zealously, therefore, all of you,
in order that you may be judged worthy
to be found within the kingdom of heaven
and to reign with Christ,
the Master of all, to whom is due all glory
with the Father and the Spirit, forever and ever. Amen.

Epilogue

The Shakers have a song that I enjoy singing, which I find demands also a dance that goes with the words:

> 'Tis the Gift to be simple, 'tis the Gift to be free,
> 'Tis the Gift to come down where we ought to be.
> And when we find ourselves in the place just right,
> 'Twill be in the valley of Love and Delight.
>
> When true Simplicity is gained
> To bow and to bend we shan't be ashamed.
> To turn, turn will be our delight,
> 'Till by turning, turning we come 'round right!

We will always be unhappy persons unless we can turn round and discover God as the center of all true love and joy. In creating his world, God meant all parts to be coordinated into a whole, into a dancing harmony. Yet, we human beings among all other material creatures are called by God to be made according to his own image and likeness (Gn 1:26-27), to share in God's inner, triune joyfulness, made to be participators of God's very own nature (2 P 1:4).

We are God's amphibious beings, called to live in intimate, joyful oneness with God dwelling within us and still live to create a harmony between ourselves and all other creatures around us. This wonderful, creating God is not only the powerful, transcendent Creator who stands above and outside of all of his creation, but he is also the immanent force that lives inside of every creature (Ac 17:28). He fills the heavens and the underworld. It is impossible to escape from his creative, sustaining Spirit (Ps 139:7).

Yet, only we human beings, endowed with free will, have the

ability to choose to live in harmony with God, the center of our obedient adoration, or to bring about disharmony within our hearts, in our relationships with the triune God, in our relationships with the rest of the cosmos. Sin has destroyed our ability to live according to God's inner rhythm, which he places within us. We have wandered "far east of Eden" looking for the face of God who alone can restore us to our lost paradise.

God's *numinous* or sacred presence was meant to be discovered within the inner depths of our being as well as inside the material layers of the world around us. We have always sought to look upon the face of God through myths and legends, symbols and sacred rituals. But sin has permeated our technical world with its own religion of matter, that has extinguished in our world the light whereby we can see God everywhere, live always in his loving presence, be joyful like happy children, as we live creatively in developing the potentials that lie dormant within us.

Entering into a sacred world

We see the need to turn "within" to make contact with a sacred presence that is more powerful than we are. We seek a sacred meaningfulness that will give ultimate direction beyond our own immediate, functional, selfish needs. Contact with this divine *source* of all beauty and lasting joy cannot be taught. It can only be evoked, awakened within our hearts by the transcendent power of God's Spirit.

It is inwardly that we must go, into our *heart*, that scriptural symbol of the interior place where we meet our Maker and Beloved in ever-expanding consciousness. This consciousness of the divine presence, as loving, uncreated energies, abiding within us and with-out us, in each material atom of the universe, grows as we tune in more consistently to listen to God's revealing Word as he speaks to us in the cosmic signs of the material universe. His Word also speaks to us and reveals God's *numinous* presence in the signs of written scripture as well as recorded history of the past and of the present moments in history now being lived and created with our cooperation. We can read these signs also inside of us in the depths of our own consciousness and unconscious.

It is therefore inside, into our *heart,* that we must go to find by the Spirit's faith, hope and love belief in God's infinite and most powerful love as manifest by Jesus Christ, the Word made flesh. We might make an attempt at moving inwardly to establish God as the center of our being. Yet, most of us come running to the surface after a short time. We miss the noise, multiplicity, the gaudy lights of the carnival and the raucous pitch of the hawker enticing us to see his side-show, "the greatest wonder on earth." The cotton candy and the sticky carnival apples delight us and make us forget what could have been.

We fear to look inwardly and honestly ask for healing from the transcendent God when we see through genuine self-knowledge what needs to be sacrificed and what needs to be transformed.

Regaining the joys of childhood

T.S. Eliot pointed out the condition we must pay to recover our lost paradise:

> A condition of complete simplicity,
> Costing not less than everything.

We have all experienced at times, perhaps when we least expected it, when we reached our "natural" rhythm. We seemed able to succeed at whatever we were doing. It was "our" day. We were really "on." It is the feeling of two persons dancing on a dance floor in synchronicity or of monks in breathless adoration of their invisible God, as they feel the rise and fall of Gregorian chant in union with the music of the ocean tides and the flight of sea gulls.

Such moments are joyous openings to the transcendent beauty of

God. We break through our "earthly" time as a measurement of length and space and come into God's eternal presence as uncontrollable life and beauty. I remember the most joyful day I ever experienced in my life. I shall never forget the sense of simplicity of God within me, around me, in all creatures. My joyous oneness that filled me with a unity of love with God as the core of my being still is vividly present to me over those past years.

This joyful at-oneness with God lasted a full twenty-four hours, all through the day and the night until the morning of the following day. There was no sleep. I was so alive to God's inner life, so full of his abundant life. Why sleep when I was so consciously aware of my being permeated in every part of my being: body, soul and spirit, with God's personalized, uncreated energies of love! Functional time disappeared, as I felt immersed in God's eternal timeliness.

There was perfect synchronicity between the transcendent Trinity, Father, Son and Spirit and myself. I was dancing with God and all the creatures of his cosmos in perfect rhythm. I was a child again, laughing with tears of joy that I never wanted to end. Yet there were also tears of sorrow, bitter-sweet. How blind of me not to have lived before in this joyous, natural rhythm, one with God and all of nature with this same awareness! How sad millions of human beings are dead to God's harmonious rhythm and live lives so deprived of this joyful, childlike abandonment to the divine source of all life! What could I do, I thought, to bring other human beings into this inner simplicity of God Trinity, calling all of his children to share the triune multiplicity in oneness.

It was too awesome an experience, that easily resisted any desire on my part to encapsulate this joyful time, in order to call it forth to enjoy against the boring and frightening aspects of future, meaningless life-situations. I have never forgotten that experience in all its vividness. But more important, the truth that sounds so clearly within me at all times since then is: The opposite of joy is not sorrow, but *disbelief.*

Jesus: our joy

Nikos Kazantzakis, the Greek writer, in his book, *St. Francis,* has the saint asking God: "Lord, where do I get the strength to sing and dance on this dunghill?" The good and joyful news of Christianity is centered on the belief of disciples of Jesus Christ that he is truly the eternal Son of God the Father. God so loved us and his world that he gave us his only Son, "so that everyone who believes in him might not perish but might have eternal life" (Jn 3:16). God's infinite goodness and love call us to share his joy by living in the Trinity's personal relationships of Father, Son and Holy Spirit, living immanently within us in an incomprehensible but total way of self-giving to us.

This is the basis for true and lasting joy, even when, as we sit on this dunghill, that permits us to sing and dance in God's rhythmic harmony. God's uncreated energies of love penetrate every part of our being. They invade us more intimately so that in him we live and move and have our being (Ac 17:28). God, as a triune community of Father, Son and Holy Spirit, lives within us in our deepest consciousness level so that in and through his incarnate Word, Jesus Christ, we can progressively become totally transformed into an ecstatic joyful oneness with him.

This reality is the end of the incarnation, death and resurrection of Jesus Christ. He came among us to make it possible, not only that we might become children of God, but that at all times we might live in that continued awareness discovered in each moment of our lives. This is our dignity: to be called children of God, and we really are such (1 Jn 3:1), in the process of discovering and surrendering to the uncreated energies of God Trinity living within us in the context of each event.

God in substance is saying to you in each moment: "Here I am; experience my love. This place is holy. Take off your shoes, your securities, and approach this burning bush to become consumed by the fire of my divine love for you."

Contemplative knowledge

This highest union, the infused union of the Trinity, in which God communicates himself as Father, Son and Spirit, is not achieved by any conceptual knowledge attained by our own efforts. It is an immediate, experiential knowledge that brings with it joy wherein the Trinity opens itself to us. God, purely and simply in his transcendence, reveals himself to you when he wishes and as he wishes. It is not that God does something new and different to you after years of your own preparation and cooperation through continued purification of your heart from self-centeredness.

But when you have cracked open the door of your heart, you stand before what was always there. You put aside your own induced disharmony to discover God's harmonious rhythm now being experienced as the *source* of new, ecstatic joy. In a state of humility you break yourself of your own power to possess your life in seeking to control both God and others. Then you enter into the reality that was always there. With Moses you have to climb up the mountain to reach God by a knowing that is an unknowing, a darkness that is truly luminous. As you separate yourself from all self-centered limitations you place on God and from all attachments to your own self-love, you gradually reach the top of the mountain.

There in the darkness of the storming clouds you hear the notes of the trumpet, and you see those lights that no human method could ever give you. No human mind, no guru, no technique could ever bring you God's personalized gift of himself, who alone can bring you lasting joy. God has to take over the communication of himself to you directly. No one but God can give himself to you through his Son as sheer gift.

Aligning yourself with God

You can change your life into one of continued joy only by pushing yourself gently to cooperate with the power and movement

of the Spirit of love to align yourself in all your being with the being
of the trinitarian, self-giving love. You then wish to do all to please
God. You desire to have no desire but to glorify God. He becomes
your "magnificent obsession." Every thought, word and deed become motivated by the desire to love God with your whole heart.
This is the primary command that Jesus calls us to obey.

It is the great dignity to which you have been called when God
created you according to the image and likeness of Christ. By striving
to become what you are in God's love, you reach the state of inner
harmony and oneness with God and neighbor and the world around
you. This is manifested in your deep joy and peace in all circumstances of your life.

Transformation by joy

By silencing the noises in your heart, you become sensitized to
listen for the "soft, kitten-like" footsteps of the Trinity walking
gently through the dense fog covering the decaying cities of your
land and the dead souls of hollow men and women. Full of childlike
power of wonder, reverence and admiration, you have new eyes to
discover "God in all things and all things in God." The heavy scales
fall from your eyes as you see God's radiant beauty and glory in his
many diaphanies or incarnations as he unfolds his infinite perfections
by wrapping himself in the external, sacramental signs of creation.

You accept God's gift of joy as you humbly trust in God's burning
love for you. You praise him working in all circumstances of your
life, because through the Spirit who has infused into you faith, hope
and love you are able joyfully to surrender to the divine energies of
love working unto your eternal happiness. You believe with Paul:
"We know that all things work for good for those who love God,
who are called according to his purpose" (Rm 8:28).

The true test of your Christian joy that must be manifested
externally to all around you, as it flows out from your experienced
union with Jesus Christ living in you, is measured by your readiness

to bear all suffering in joy. Such perfect joy has been well described in the story of Francis of Assisi who spoke to Brother Leo, as they returned to their friary after a journey:

> And if we continue to knock at the door and the brother porter comes out and drives us away with curses and hard blows—and if we bear it patiently, and take the insults with joy and love in our hearts, Oh, Brother Leo, write down that that is perfect joy!

Paul provides us with the best description of Christian joy that can fittingly summarize this book:

> What then shall we say to this? If God is for us, who can be against us? He who did not spare his own Son but handed him over for us all, how will he not also give us everything else along with him? . . . It is Christ Jesus who died, rather, was raised, who also is at the right hand of God, who indeed intercedes for us. What will separate us from the love of Christ? Will anguish, or distress, or persecution, or famine, or nakedness, or peril, or the sword? . . . No, in all these things we conquer overwhelmingly through him who loved us. For I am convinced that neither death, nor life, nor angels, nor principalities, nor present things, nor future things, nor powers, nor heights, nor depth, nor any other creature will be able to separate us from the love of God in Christ Jesus our Lord. (Rm 8:31-39)

Select Bibliography

Bermejo, Luis M. *The Spirit of Life: The Holy Spirit in the Life of the Christian.* Chicago: Loyola University Press, 1989.

Bernard of Clairvaux. *Tractatus de gradibus humilitatis et superbiae.* Patrologia Latina, vol. 182. Edited by J. P. Migne.

Bovenmars, Jan G. *Biblical Spirituality of the Heart.* Staten Island, New York: Alba House, 1991.

Braun, F. M. *Mother of God's People.* Staten Island, New York: Alba House, 1967.

Carol, Juniper B., ed. *Mariology.* Milwaukee: Bruce, 1957.

Cassian, John. *Conferences.* Translated by Colm Luibheid, Classics of Western Spirituality. Mahway, New Jersey: Paulist Press, 1985.

Caussade, J. P. de *Self-Abandonment to Divine Providence.* Garden City, New York: Doubleday Co., 1975.

Chardin, Pierre Teilhard de. *The Divine Milieu.* Translated by W. Wall. New York: Harper & Row, 1960.

_____. *The Future of Man.* Translated by N. Denny. New York: Harper & Row, 1964.

Climacus, John. *The Ladder of Divine Ascent.* Translated by Lazarus Moore. London: Faber & Faber, 1959.

Congar, Yves M. J. *I Believe in the Holy Spirit.* 3 vols. Translated by David Smith. New York: The Seabury Press, 1983.

Durckheim, Karlfried, Graf von. *The Way of Transformation.* London: Unwin Paperbacks, 1980.

Durrwell, F. X. *The Resurrection.* 2d ed. Translated by Rosemary Sheed. New York: Sheed & Ward, 1960.

Evely, Louis. *Joy.* Translated by Brian and Marie-Claude Thompson. New York: Herder & Herder, 1967.

French, R., transl. *The Way of a Pilgrim.* New York: Ballantine, 1977.

Fuller, Reginald H. *The Foundations of New Testament Christology.* New York: Charles Scribner's Sons, 1965.

Graham, Billy. *Angels: God's Secret Agents.* Garden City, New York: Doubleday & Co., 1975.

Hausherr, Irenee. *Penthos—la doctrine de la componction dans l'Orient chrétien. Orientalia Christiana Analecta.* No. 132. Rome: Pontifical Oriental Institute, 1944.

Hilary of Poitiers. *The Trinity.* Translated by Stephen McKenna. The Fathers of the Church Series, vol. 25. Washington, D.C.: Catholic University Press, 1954.

Hunt, Gladys M. *Don't Be Afraid to Die.* Grand Rapids, Michigan: Zondervan, 1971.

Isaac the Syrian. *Mystic Treatises.* Translated by A. J. Wensinck. Amsterdam: Niewe Reeks, 1969.

Lossky, V. *The Mystical Theology of the Eastern Church.* Cambridge & London: James Clarke & Co., Ltd., 1957.

Maloney, George A. *Bright Darkness: Jesus—the Lover of Mankind.* Denville, New Jersey: Dimension Books, 1977.

_____. *Communion of Saints.* Hauppauge, New York: Living Flame Press, 1988.

_____. *The Cosmic Christ, from Paul to Teilhard.* New York: Sheed & Ward, 1968.

_____. *Death, Where Is Your Sting?* Staten Island, New York: Alba House, 1984.

_____. *The Everlasting Now.* Notre Dame, Indiana: Ave Maria Press, 1980.

_____. *The First Day of Eternity: Resurrection Now.* New York: Crossroad, 1982.

_____. *In Jesus We Trust.* Notre Dame, Indiana: Ave Maria Press, 1990.

_____. *Invaded by God: Mysticism & the Indwelling Trinity.* Denville, New Jersey: Dimension Books, 1979.

_____. *Mary, the Womb of God.* Denville, New Jersey: Dimension Books, 1976.

_____. *Mysticism and the New Age: Christic Consciousness in the New Creation.* Staten Island, New York: Alba House, 1991.

_____. *The Spirit Broods Over the World.* Staten Island, New York: Alba House, 1993.

Martin, Malachi. *Jesus Now.* New York: E. P. Dutton & Co., Inc., 1973.

McKenzie, John L. "Angels." *Dictionary of the Bible.* New York: Bruce Co., 1965, 30-32.

Merton, Thomas. *Seeds of Contemplation.* Norfolk: Dell Books, 1949.

_____. *New Seeds of Contemplation.* New York: New Direction Books, 1962.

Moltmann, Jurgen. *Theology of Hope.* New York: Harper & Row, 1967.

Murray, Andrew. *Humility: the Beauty of Holiness.* Old Tappan, New Jersey: Fleming H. Revell Co., undated.

Nee, Watchman. *The Joyful Heart.* Wheaton, Illinois: Tyndale House, 1985.

Panikkar, Raimundo. *The Trinity and the Religious Experience of Man.* New York: Orbis Books, 1973.

Pannenberg, Wolfhart. *Jesus—God and Man.* Translated by Lewis L. Wilking and Decane A. Priebe. Philadelphia: The Westminster Press, 1968.

Rahner, Karl. *Mary, Mother of the Lord.* New York: Sheed & Ward, 1963.

_____. *The Trinity.* New York: Herder & Herder, 1969.

_____. *On the Theology of Death.* Translated by C. H. Henkey. New York: Herder & Herder, 1961.

Ramsey, A. M. *The Resurrection of Christ.* London: G. Bles, 1945.

Scheeben, M. J. *The Mysteries of Christianity.* Translated by Cyril Vollert. St. Louis: B. Herder Book Co., 1946.

Schillebeeckx, E. *Mary, Mother of the Redemption.* New York: Sheed & Ward, 1964.

_____. *Sacramental Reconciliation.* Concilium Series. New York: Herder & Herder, 1971.

Schoonenberg, P. *Man and Sin.* Translated by Joseph Donceel. Notre Dame, Indiana: University of Notre Dame Press, 1965.

Symeon the New Theologian: *The Hymns of Divine Love.* Translated by George A. Maloney. Denville, New Jersey: Dimension Books, 1974.

Toynbee A. *et al. Man's Concern with Death.* New York: McGraw-Hill, 1969.

Van Zeller, Hubert. *The Inner Search.* New York: Sheed & Ward, 1957.

Vann, Gerald. *The Heart of Man.* Garden City, New York: Doubleday Co., 1962.

Vogel, Arthur A. *The Power of His Resurrection.* New York: Seabury Press, 1976.

Weaver, Bertrand. *Joy.* New York: Sheed & Ward, 1964.

Williams, Esther. *The Heart of Salvation: the Life and Teachings of St. Theophan the Recluse.* Newbury, Massachusetts: Praxis Institute Press, 1992.